WHAT TO DO WHEN YOU DON'T HAVE $500

SURVIVING THE BILLS THAT WON'T WAIT AND THE CASH THAT ISN'T THERE

CARL WILLIAMS

Publisher's Note

Inkylines & Words LLC is an independent creative press founded by Carl "Will" Williams in Yokohama, Japan, and registered in Honolulu, Hawaii. We publish works that illuminate resilience, belonging, and the quiet art of becoming whole again. Our mission is to create stories, guides, and reflections that help readers find strength and meaning in the places where light almost seems to fade.

To explore new releases or connect with the author, visit https://payhip.com/inkylinesandwords.

DEDICATION

For everyone in the struggle right now.

For those who've stared at a stack of bills with nothing left but grit.
For the nights you went hungry so your kids didn't.
For the mornings you faced the world with an empty wallet,
And the days you kept working when exhaustion begged you to quit.

This is for the fighters the world overlooks.
You are more than the numbers in your account.
Survival is a form of courage that the wealthy may never understand.

You are not alone.
You are not invisible.

WORDS OF COMFORT

If you're holding this book, chances are life has put you in a hard place. Maybe the bills came faster than the paycheck. Maybe an emergency wiped out what little you had saved. Maybe you're staring at an empty fridge, wondering how to stretch a handful of coins into tomorrow. If that's you, hear this first:

You are not a failure. You are not lazy. You are not broken.

The world tells us that money equals worth, but it doesn't. You are worth more than your bank balance, more than your debts, more than the shame you've been made to feel. Struggling financially doesn't make you less. Surviving without enough makes you stronger than most will ever know.

You are not alone.

Millions of people, workers, parents, students, and grandparents are walking this same tightrope every day, quietly fighting to make it through the week. Some hide it out of fear. Some carry it in silence. But the struggle is everywhere. If you've ever felt invisible in that fight, let this book remind you: you are seen.

This book will not judge you. It won't lecture you from a mountaintop. It will meet you right where you are in the panic, in the late notices, in the "I don't know how to make it through this week." It offers actions you can take today, not someday. Step by step, we'll move from panic to calm, from empty to enough, and eventually, from surviving to something more meaningful.

Take a breath. You've already done the most challenging part: you kept going. That means you're still in the fight. And now, you don't have to fight alone.

PREFACE

For the moments when the floor disappears beneath you.

No one plans for the day the math stops working. When the check doesn't come, when the bill doubles, when the card declines in a grocery line that suddenly feels too bright, you tell yourself you'll figure it out. But fear doesn't wait for logic. It tightens your chest, fogs your thoughts, and makes the simplest tasks feel like lifting stone.

This book isn't about advice. It's about steadiness when advice isn't enough. It's about the smallest movements, the kind you make when everything feels too heavy to lift at once. It won't promise miracles, but it will offer motion. It will remind you there's always one more thing to try, one more corner to check, one more call to make.

You'll meet voices that don't speak from comfort. They speak from basements and borrowed couches, from nights that ended with nothing but the will to try again. They learned that control doesn't come back all at once. It returns in quiet, deliberate choices.

There's no shame in where you are. Brokenness isn't a condition; it's a moment between what was and what can be rebuilt. What's inside these pages isn't a rescue plan. It's a series of handholds carved from experienced ways to catch yourself before the fall steepens, ways to turn surviving into breathing space.

What follows is divided into three parts: the shock of losing footing, the strain of scraping by, and the slow rebuilding that becomes a source of strength. Each stage has its rhythm: panic, persistence, and peace. You won't face them all at once. You'll take them as life gives them to you, one step at a time.

Read this however you need to. Start where you are. Skip what doesn't fit. This isn't a book that demands to be finished; it's one meant to stay open, a companion for the days that test you and the mornings that ask you to try again.

If you're holding this, you've already done the hardest thing: you refused to disappear. Let these pages remind you what that means. You're not waiting for rescue, you're learning to rise, slowly and thoroughly, until you remember your own strength.

And when you finish, let it end where all recovery begins, not with perfection, but with presence. You're here. That's enough.

You can't control the fall, but you can choose how to rise.

This book won't promise ease; it will teach you how to stand again, slowly and thoroughly, until you remember your own strength.

CONTENTS

PART I: THE BREAKING POINT 1

CHAPTER 1: The $500 Cliff: Why So Many Fall Here 3

CHAPTER 2: When the Bills Break You — First 24 Hours of Panic 7

CHAPTER 3: Wallets Like Empty Rooms — Facing Zero Cash 12

CHAPTER 4: Coins on the Table — Finding Money You Forgot You Had 16

CHAPTER 5: Selling the Invisible — Turning Stuff Into Survival Cash 20

PART II: SCRAPING BY 25

CHAPTER 6: Bread and Beans — Food That Fills for Under $2 a Day 28

CHAPTER 7: The Call That Cuts Your Bill in Half — Scripts That Work 33

CHAPTER 8: Leaky Buckets — Stopping Payday Loans, Overdrafts, and Traps 36

CHAPTER 9: The Rent Wall: What to Do When Shelter Is at Risk 40

CHAPTER 10: Wheels on Fumes — Surviving Transportation Without Cash 44

CHAPTER 11: Cold Nights, Dark Rooms — Surviving Utilities When They're Cut Off 48

PART III: THE HUMAN WEIGHT 53

CHAPTER 12: Shame Is a Debt You Don't Owe — Breaking the Silence 56

CHAPTER 13: The Hidden Hands — Churches, Charities, and Mutual Aid 60

CHAPTER 14: Alone at the Table — Surviving the Mental Crash 63

CHAPTER 15: Hungry Children, Heavy Hearts — Holding the Family Together ... 67

CHAPTER 16: The Neighbor's Knock — Asking for Help Without Losing Yourself 71

PART IV: FROM BROKE TO BREATHING 75

CHAPTER 17: The First Buffer — Building Your $500 Lifeline 78

CHAPTER 18: Small Sparks — Turning Gig Cash Into Stability 82

CHAPTER 19: When Rest Becomes Work — Fighting Burnout While You Build Back 85
CHAPTER 20: The Slow Rise — Building a Life That Doesn't Break Again 89
CHAPTER 21: The Living Ledger — Keeping What You've Rebuilt from Breaking Again 93
CHAPTER 22: The Quiet Proof — When You No Longer Have to Explain Survival 97

NOTES & SOURCES 101

RECOMMENDED READING AND FINANCIAL AID RESOURCES 103

AFTERWORD / AUTHOR'S NOTE 105

ACKNOWLEDGMENTS 107

ABOUT THE AUTHOR 108

PART I

THE BREAKING POINT

No one plans to break. It happens in a blink: the job loss, the missed payment, the unexpected hit that pulls the floor out from under you. Panic doesn't knock; it floods. In these moments, survival begins not with solutions, but with breath. This part is about that first breath, the raw one that hurts but still counts. You're not fixing anything yet. You're learning how to steady your hands when everything you built begins to crumble.

This is where survival starts, not in calm days when everything balances, but in the nights when panic presses against your chest, and numbers refuse to work. The Breaking Point is the edge where paychecks vanish, but bills keep coming, where a single flat tire or medical bill can tilt a family into freefall. It's where shame whispers that you've failed, even though millions stand in the same storm.

At the breaking point, fear takes the wheel. You refresh the banking app, hoping the balance has changed. You avoid calls because you already know the number on the screen wants money you don't have. You tell yourself it's temporary, but anxiety doesn't wait. It pounds at the door, demanding decisions before you've had time to think.

This section is about catching yourself before panic makes the worst decisions. Because survival rarely collapses in one blow, it unravels through payday loans, overdraft fees, and silence that costs more than speaking up. A crisis convinces you that every bill is urgent. The truth: some can wait. Food and shelter cannot.

Here, you'll find tools for those first dangerous days. No advice about skipping lattes. Not lectures about savings you don't have. Just moves you can make in the next hour, the next day, the next week. These chapters will show you how to breathe when panic floods your body. How to sort broken bones from paper cuts in your finances. How to scrape together coins and credits you forgot you had. How to turn "nothing" into just enough to last until tomorrow.

You'll meet people who've been exactly where you are. Maria, who ignored one bill and paid hundreds in penalties before she learned to call first. James, who thought silence bought time but discovered it only bought court fees. Angela, who found food for her family by checking a forgotten app balance. Their stories prove the breaking point isn't the end. It's the start of endurance.

The Breaking Point is not a verdict. It's a threshold. These first steps won't fix everything. But they'll stop the freefall. They'll buy you time. They'll give you footholds, small, uneven, sometimes humiliating, but always proof that you're not powerless.

Take a breath. This section is about survival in motion, about halting the slide long enough to regroup. Before we can rebuild, we have to stop the fall. That's what Part I delivers.

CHAPTER 1

THE $500 CLIFF: WHY SO MANY FALL HERE

Five hundred dollars. That's the threshold, the point where half of America is hanging on by a thread. One minor setback: a flat tire, a co-pay, a rent hike, and the drop begins. It may not sound like much, but when you don't have it, everything changes.

A flat tire. A doctor's bill. A utility deposit. These aren't headline disasters, but inside a household, they hit like earthquakes. They rattle the fragile balance between bills and groceries, the rhythm of work and home.

Half of U.S. households can't cover a $500 emergency. And it's not just the visibly poor. Families who seem stable, office workers, parents, and even college graduates are one missed paycheck away from collapse. The danger hides in plain sight, right at the dinner table, buried in unopened envelopes.

Why $500? Because margins have shrunk to the bone. Wages stay flat while rent climbs. Groceries rise each week. Paychecks stretch, but they don't bend. A few hundred dollars isn't "extra." It's the difference between floating and drowning.

Here's the truth: falling short of $500 doesn't mean you've failed. It doesn't mean you're careless or reckless. The usual advice to budget better, save more, and skip the coffee misses the point. Crisis doesn't come from lattes.

It comes from rent spikes, medical bills, car repairs, and jobs that don't cover both living and surviving.

This isn't about your worth. It's about a system built without Slack. Payday loans, overdraft fees, and late charges aren't accidents. They're traps. The economy profits when you stumble.

And yet, you're here, reading. That means you haven't given up. Endurance takes a kind of courage. It doesn't look glamorous. It looks like stretching rice over three days. Like choosing which bill to pay just to keep the lights on. Like dragging yourself to work when exhaustion begs you to stop. That isn't a weakness. That's grit.

Maria knows this edge too well. She worked two jobs until her son broke his arm. The co-pay was $600. That single incident triggered overdrafts, late fees, and eventually a payday loan. She sat in the dark, shut-off notice in her lap, watching one fracture unravel everything. Maria's story isn't rare. It's the quiet reality for millions.

And Maria isn't alone. Kevin once sold the only set of tools he had left, heirlooms from his father, to buy three days' worth of groceries. He cried afterward. Not because the food didn't matter, but because the sale reminded him how quickly stability can vanish. That's the $500 cliff: the sudden shift from steady to desperate, with nothing in between.

Shame makes the edge sharper. It tells you the drop is your fault. But millions stand here with you, workers, parents, students, grandparents. They don't talk about it because silence feels safer. That silence convinces everyone they're alone. You aren't.

Sometimes, strength looks like lifelines. James dug $20 from a jar of spare change. It bought bread, eggs, and peanut butter. Tasha used a forgotten $10 gift card to buy cereal and milk. Luis sold old textbooks for $18 and turned them into pasta and sauce enough for a week of meals. Kevin traded his tools for groceries. These aren't miracles. They're footholds.

The precipice doesn't discriminate. Teachers fall. Nurses fall. Parents juggling two jobs fall. The edge doesn't care how hard you worked last month; it waits for the slightest slip.

The first step to surviving broke weeks is naming the problem. Once you do, the lie that "falling means you're less" begins to lose its grip. This isn't your flaw. It's the system's. And once you recognize that, you stop wasting energy on shame and start directing it toward action.

This book won't waste your time with lectures about skipping coffee. Instead, you'll find real steps: how to eat on less than $2 a day, how to keep a roof over your head when rent feels impossible, and how to find cash in 24 hours without falling into payday traps. Step by step, we'll move from broke weeks to breathing room.

If you're standing at the $500 edge right now, listen: you're not weak, and you're not alone. The drop is real. So is the climb back. You've already endured more than most. Now it's time to think smarter with strategies that work during panic, not just in theory.

Take a breath. Mark today as the start. This isn't the end. It's your first foothold.

The next danger comes fast, the first 24 hours after the bills hit, when panic pushes you toward the worst choices. That's where we go next.

Emergency Moves

- **Name the edge**

  Say it out loud: *"This isn't about my worth. It's the $500 cliff, and I'm not the only one here."*

- **Face the number**

  Write down only the urgent bills: rent, food, and utilities. Circle the total. This is what matters first.

- **Take inventory**

  Count every coin, every dollar, and every resource: pantry items, hours you can trade, favors you can call in. Small stacks add up.

- **Mark the starting line**

  Write today's date. Call it the day you stopped drowning and began climbing.

CHAPTER 2

WHEN THE BILLS BREAK YOU — FIRST 24 HOURS OF PANIC

A knock. An envelope stamped in red. A text from the bank: *balance negative*. Panic doesn't wait politely. It slams into your chest before you finish reading. In seconds, your week unravels.

The first 24 hours after a setback are the most dangerous. Fear pushes you toward payday loans, overdraft "protection," and buy-now-pay-later schemes. Anxiety convinces you that every bill must be paid immediately. But not everything is urgent, even when it feels that way.

Think of this stage as triage. In an emergency room, broken bones are treated before paper cuts. Food, shelter, electricity, and the phone you need for work, those are your basics. Credit cards, streaming services, even some medical bills? Paper cuts. Address the bones first. Without them, the patient doesn't make it.

Step One: Breathe

Before you do anything, breathe.
Inhale. Hold. Exhale. Repeat.

Write it down if you need to: *Breathe before you move.*
Air is free, and it clears the fog. Panic narrows vision. Breathing widens it.

Step Two: Get Clear

Bills grow into monsters when they live in your head. Drag them into daylight.

Write each one down, then split them into two groups:

- **Survival:** Rent, food, lights, phone for work.
- **Delay:** Credit cards, gym memberships, subscriptions.

On paper, the chaos shrinks. It becomes manageable.

Step Three: Make the Call

This is where many stumble. Shame tells you to hide. But hiding costs more.

Maria once ignored her light bill, and the power company shut off her service. A $75 reconnection fee pushed her deeper into debt. Two months later, she fell behind again. This time, she called before the account defaulted. The representative split her payment and gave her ten extra days. One call kept her lights on.

James stayed silent after receiving an eviction notice. He thought waiting one more day wouldn't matter. But court fees stacked up, and his landlord refused partial payment. Silence turned late rent into a crisis.

Angela expected humiliation when she called her gas company. Instead, they gave her a two-week extension. Ten minutes bought her fourteen days of heat.

DeShawn scraped together $15 and called his water provider. They accepted it as a good-faith payment and gave him a one-week grace period. Fifteen dollars bought him water and time.

And Rosa? She owed her phone carrier $180. Losing service would mean losing her job. She called, offered $25, and asked for options. They cut her late fees in half and set up a payment plan. Without that call, her phone and her paycheck would have disappeared.

When you call, skip the speeches. One line is enough:

"I want to pay, but I can't cover the full amount this week. What options do I have to avoid shutoff or fees?"

That sentence has saved thousands.

Step Four: Send Something

Even a token payment can buy breathing room. Twenty dollars toward a $200 balance might seem pointless, but companies notice effort. Action signals commitment. Pride won't keep the fridge cold. A small payment might.

Step Five: Avoid the Traps

This is the moment when quick fixes tempt hardest. Payday loans promise fast cash. Overdraft "protection" looks like a lifeline. Buy-now-pay-later options break bills into neat little chunks. But these aren't lifelines, they're traps with receipts. Every borrowed dollar returns with friends: fees, penalties, and interest.

Rule one of broke weeks is simple:
Don't dig deeper while trying to climb out.

Step Six: Guard Your Mind

The first day of crisis doesn't just attack your wallet; it attacks your mind. Anger, shame, and despair pile on. You want to crawl under the covers and shut it all out. That instinct is natural, but it worsens the spiral.

Here's the truth: you've been here before. You've stretched meals, juggled deadlines, borrowed, hustled, scraped by. You're still standing. That means you already know how to fight through storms.

Terror shouts, *"No way out."*
Endurance whispers, *"One move at a time."*

Each move is a foothold. Stack enough footholds, and you stop sliding.

The First 24 Hours Are About Momentum

Breathe. List. Call. Send. Resist traps. Guard your mind.
Do those, and you've turned panic into progress.

Emergency Moves Recap

- **Breathe first**. Inhale, hold, exhale. Write *"Breathe before you move"* somewhere visible.
- **List everything**. Put bills on paper. Label **survival** expenses (rent, food, lights, work phone) vs **delay** payments (cards, loans, subscriptions).
- **Call early**. Use this line:
  "I want to pay, but can't cover the full amount this week. What options do I have to avoid shutoff or fees?"
- **Send something**. Even $20 shows effort. Pair it with a call.

- **Avoid traps**. Skip payday loans, overdrafts, and buy-now-pay-later. They make next week harder.
- **Guard your mind**. Recognize fear as part of the fight. Name it, then act anyway.

CHAPTER 3

WALLETS LIKE EMPTY ROOMS — FACING ZERO CASH

You open your wallet, and it mocks you, no coins, no bills, just silence. Then the banking app confirms it: zero or worse, a negative balance. That silence doesn't sit still. It screams. In that moment, life feels like it's running on fumes.

Zero isn't just a number. It's a weight pressing on your chest with every thought of tonight's meal and tomorrow's needs. Fear insists there's nothing left. Shame whispers that you've already failed.

But nothing almost always hides *something*.
And so, the hunt begins.

The Hunt Begins

Start with what's closest, empty every pocket, jacket, jeans, and backpack. Check the car console, couch cushions, and old jars. It may feel beneath you, but hunger is louder than pride.

People routinely scrape together twenty, fifty, or even a hundred dollars this way. That's not shame. That's groceries.

- Tasha found four dollars in coins beneath her bed. It bought bread and ramen for two days of meals.

- Malik pulled forty-two dollars from an old duffel bag. It carried him through the week.
- Rosa uncovered two gift cards worth eighteen dollars. They became milk, cereal, and fruit.

None of these were miracles. They were proof that survival often hides in plain sight.

Digital Leftovers

Next, go online. Log in to PayPal, Cash App, Venmo, or store rewards apps. Search your email for words like *"refund," "credit,"* or *"rebate."* Check loyalty programs. Gift card balances often sit untouched.

Even five dollars can mean dinner.

- Andre found $3.78 in PayPal enough for peanut butter and bread.
- Angela opened an old store app and found a $25 credit. It paid for diapers and baby food.
- Marcus didn't check. Payday felt close. By the weekend, hunger pushed him into a payday loan that doubled his debt.

Doing nothing costs more than the few dollars he overlooked.

Selling Small, Fast

When the apps run dry, turn to what you own. Pawn shops, kiosks, and resale apps don't care about pride; they care about possessions.

- Angela pawned a broken laptop for $25. It covered her bus fare for two weeks.
- Chris sold a box of DVDs for twelve dollars. It bought groceries and time.

Small sales add up. A handful of used books. A board game. An old toaster oven. Ten or twenty dollars here and there.

It won't pay rent. But it will feed you tonight.

Every sale is proof you're still moving forward.

Work With Your Hands

If there's nothing left to sell, use your body and your skills. Babysit, mow lawns, wash cars, carry groceries, clean garages, walk dogs, tutor kids, or deliver food. Your community always needs helping hands. Payment might come in cash, meals, or bus fare; every form matters.

When DeShawn ran out of options, he cleaned a neighbor's garage for fifteen dollars and a bag of groceries. That single afternoon stretched his week. Janelle braids her friend's daughter's hair for twenty bucks, which covers lunch and gas until payday.

The labor may seem small, but it creates momentum when your bank account is stuck at zero.

Claim Hidden Credits

Sometimes, money isn't gone, it's just sitting where you left it. Utilities, banks, and insurance companies often hold deposits or overpayments. Call and ask. Even fifteen dollars from an old account is better in your pocket than theirs. A five-minute phone call could mean groceries tonight.

Advances

Some employers will release part of your paycheck early if you explain your situation. Gig apps like Uber, DoorDash, and Instacart often pay daily. Even thirty or fifty dollars can reset the clock. It's not about fixing everything; it's about buying time.

Guard Your Mind

The real danger of zero isn't an empty wallet, it's the voice that says you're finished. That lie weighs more than hunger. But you've been broke before. You stretched scraps into meals, borrowed when needed, hustled wherever you could. And you're still here. That alone proves emptiness isn't the end.

An empty wallet doesn't mean empty hands; it means the hunt begins again. Every coin, dollar, and credit you find is a step back from the edge. Progress isn't jackpots. It's tiny victories stacked until you can breathe again.

The world says zero means nothing. But look at what you've already done with nothing. You found scraps and made them stretch, turned panic into patience, and called hunger by its real name: survival. You are proof that even when the math says "impossible," the heart keeps adding up to more. You are not empty. You are a resource.

CHAPTER 4

COINS ON THE TABLE — FINDING MONEY YOU FORGOT YOU HAD

Being broke doesn't always mean you're empty. Sometimes, it means your money is hiding in credits, refunds, deposits, or balances you've overlooked. A single coin can buy food. A refund check can keep the lights on. These aren't strokes of luck; they're signs of strategy.

A Search-and-Rescue Mission

Think of this like a search-and-rescue operation. You're not flailing in panic; you're moving with intention, turning over cushions, scrolling through old accounts, pressing companies not from desperation, but with strategy. The treasure isn't gold bars. It's a crumpled bill in a drawer, a fifteen-dollar rebate, or a forgotten app balance. Every overlooked dollar adds up to a meal, a tank of gas, or a day's peace of mind.

Forgotten Balances

Start with the easy wins. Everyone has them: gift cards tucked in drawers, loyalty points hiding in pharmacy apps, or airline miles that can convert into gift cards. Log in to PayPal, Cash App, or Venmo. Search your inbox for refund notices. Even five dollars can cover bread or bus fare. Small amounts feel meaningless until they feed you.

Angela once logged into a dusty pharmacy app and found thirty-two dollars in rewards. She turned it into groceries, three full meals from digital dust. Malik discovered an unused ten-dollar Amazon credit and bought diapers. That scrap of digital money bought him another week of breathing space.

Returns That Feed You

Next, scan your home. Clothes with tags, unopened gadgets, and kitchenware still in boxes are untapped resources. Many stores offer refunds or store credit, even without receipts. That credit turns into groceries, gas, or cleaning supplies.

One woman returned a $20 set of headphones and walked out with three days of food. Rosa exchanged a fifteen-dollar holiday mug set for paper towels and pasta. Neither win was glamorous. Both meant survival.

Push further. Bottles and cans with deposits pile up in garages. Ten cents here, fifteen there, they add up at the redemption center. Old electronics can earn cash. Textbooks can be sold back. Unwanted gifts become store credit. You're not just decluttering. You're converting dead weight into fuel.

Company Deposits and Refunds

Now, step outside your home. Utility companies often require deposits when you first set up service, and if you've moved, they might still be holding yours. Call your former gas, water, electric, internet, and phone providers. Do the same with your insurance companies. Overpayments and rebates can go unclaimed for years. A ten-minute call could put fifty dollars or more back in your pocket.

Malik contacted his old water company and found they owed him $75 from a deposit. He picked it up the next day. That money covered a week of groceries and lifted a weight he hadn't realized was pressing down on him.

Banks and Unclaimed Property

Banks also hold forgotten balances in dormant accounts. Even twelve or fifteen dollars belongs to you, not them. Some banks eventually transfer these balances to the state through a process called *escheatment.* Once that happens, claiming your money becomes harder. So call the bank first.

Don't overlook state unclaimed property databases, either. Every state holds billions in refunds, paychecks, and deposits that never reached their owners. Maybe a final paycheck was mailed to the wrong address. Maybe a utility deposit wasn't forwarded. A quick name search can show what's waiting. (Search online for "unclaimed property + [your state]" to find the official site.) Some people find hundreds of dollars this way. But even twenty-five dollars matters when your fridge is bare.

Lena searched her state's site and found $87 in unclaimed property, plus $15 on a gift card and $32 in pharmacy rewards. That $134 paid for groceries, gas, and three days of breathing room.

Proof in Small Victories

Andre cashed out $3.78 from PayPal and bought bread and peanut butter. It carried him through the night. Tasha slid a worn Walmart gift card across the counter and left with cereal and milk. Her kids ate breakfast because of $9.44.

These wins range from a few dollars to hundreds. They won't erase rent or wipe out debt, but they prove something shame hides: you're not powerless. Momentum is the real gift. Every time you recover money, three dollars in an app, twenty from returns, seventy-five in deposits, you prove that movement is possible.

Broke weeks feel heavy because they pin you down. Finding hidden money breaks that weight. Getting through isn't about jackpots. It's about stacking scraps into time. And time is the currency that lets you keep fighting.

Emergency Moves

- **Check gift cards and apps.** Use forgotten balances, loyalty rewards, or points. Even three dollars feeds you.
- **Return unused items**: Clothes, gadgets, unopened groceries. Trade clutter for essentials today.
- **Call utilities and carriers.** Ask about deposits or credits from past accounts.
- **Check banks and insurance.** Dormant balances and overpayments belong to you.
- **Search state databases.** Claim unclaimed paychecks, rebates, or deposits.
- **Cancel and request refunds.** End subscriptions or memberships you don't need.

CHAPTER 5

SELLING THE INVISIBLE — TURNING STUFF INTO SURVIVAL CASH

Stop. Look around. You may feel broke, but you're surrounded by money in disguise, phones tucked in drawers, shoes you never wear, gadgets gathering dust, and a chair no one uses. Staying afloat starts with recognizing it, valuing it, and turning it into cash.

More Than "Nothing"

When you're broke, "nothing" can feel true. But it rarely is. The problem isn't usually absence, it's blindness: not seeing the value in what's already around you. The key is speed. Forget top dollar. You need survival dollars. Cash today keeps the lights on. Waiting for perfect prices leads to shutoff notices and eviction letters.

Electronics First

Old phones, tablets, laptops, and consoles lose value every year. But pawn shops, kiosks, and resale apps will still buy them even if they're cracked or outdated. That iPhone sitting in your drawer isn't worth memories; it's worth $40 in your hand today.

Angela pawned a broken laptop for $25. That covered two weeks of bus fare. Progress, not profit. Marcus sold three old gaming controllers online for $18.

It wasn't rent money, but it filled his gas tank and got him to work. That $18 mattered more than nostalgia.

Jordan, a college student, sold his cracked Xbox for $50 using a same-day app. It wasn't glamorous, but it bought him groceries and printer ink for his assignments. Even broken electronics carry survival value.

Clothes and Shoes

When the electronics are gone, open the closet. Not just for fashionable pieces, work boots, winter coats, uniforms, and children's clothing sell fast because they meet real needs. A bag of kids' clothes brought in $15. A pair of steel-toed boots sold for $30. That's groceries or gas.

Tonya sold three outgrown winter coats her kids had outgrown. She got $28 and used part of it for groceries, smaller jackets, and warm meals for the week.

Luis found a pair of sneakers he hadn't worn since high school. He listed them online and earned $22 in a day. That single sale bought lunches for an entire week.

Furniture and Appliances

A $20 microwave or a $30 chair may not seem valuable. But to someone else, it's a bargain. To you, it's dinner. List items cheaply on Facebook Marketplace, Craigslist, or local buy/sell apps. If they don't sell within 48 hours, lower the price or consider pawning them. Quick money beats waiting for top dollar.

Kevin sold his stained couch for $40. A college student wanted it. That $40 kept his lights on for another week. Denise sold a battered dresser for $15.

The cash covered soap, toothpaste, and bus fare. Furniture that looked useless became survival.

Scrap and Micro-Sales

Look past the obvious. Recycling centers pay for scrap metal, aluminum cans even broken bikes. DeShawn gathered soda cans and turned them into $8, enough for three days of ramen and eggs.

Small items count too: books, DVDs, costume jewelry, board games, and kitchen gadgets. Chris sold a box of DVDs for $12, enough for a week of bus fare. Rosa pawned costume jewelry she'd never worn for $22, which covered groceries and gas.

Angela cleaned out her kitchen drawers and sold a used blender for $10. That $10 stretched into three nights of meals: rice, beans, and tortillas. Little sales don't sound heroic, but they add up fast.

Barter Works Too

When the items run out, trade your skills. Cash isn't the only currency. A neighbor might exchange groceries for babysitting. Someone could trade gas money for your old bike. Yard work might get you dinner.

Derrick mowed lawns in exchange for rides to work. For two weeks, he cut grass and got daily lifts that kept his job secure. His wallet stayed thin, but his income didn't vanish.

Maria, a single mom, swapped weekend babysitting for grocery bags from her neighbor. She hated needing the help, but her kids ate. In broke weeks, barter is survival in action.

The Cost of Letting Go

Letting go hurts a jacket once loved, a TV once cherished, a gadget once saved for. It feels like surrender. But jackets don't pay bills. Gadgets don't keep the heat on. Cash does.

Maya sold an old TV for $40. It didn't cover rent, but it bought four days of groceries. That $40 kept her from taking out a payday loan. Kevin's couch, Marcus's controllers, and Rosa's jewelry weren't miracles, but each proved that letting go can mean holding on.

Real failure isn't selling. Real failure is clinging to things while the lights go dark. Pride doesn't feed you. Cash does. Every sale buys time to eat, breathe, and plan your next move.

Emergency Moves

- **Sell electronics: fast** phones, tablets, laptops, consoles. Pawn or sell via apps today.
- **Move clothes and shoes,** coats, uniforms, boots, and kids' gear are always in demand.
- **Unload furniture and appliances** at a low price to sell within 24–48 hours.
- **Bundle small items**: DVDs, books, jewelry, gadgets. $10 here, $20 there adds up.
- **Collect scrap and cans,** trade metal, tools, or recyclables for quick money.
- **Barter labor**, babysit, mow, clean, or trade gear for food or rides.
- Price to move fast cash beats maximum profit. Sell quickly, move forward.

PART II
SCRAPING BY

You've survived the first fall. The panic has passed, but the silence that follows hits harder. This is where exhaustion replaces fear, where every decision feels heavier, every step slower. It's not the chaos of breaking; it's the ache of continuing. What comes next isn't about rescue. It's about endurance, the quiet, unglamorous kind that turns survival into skill. This section will guide you through moving forward, stretching what you have, and holding on until movement becomes momentum again.

If you're still here, it means you survived the fall. You've already faced the hardest part: the shock. You stared down panic, opened envelopes stamped in red, and watched your bank app blink back an empty screen. Yet somehow, you're still standing. That alone proves you've already done what shame said you couldn't endure.

Now comes the grind. Scraping by doesn't roar. It drags. It's not a single storm but a slow leak, quiet, constant, relentless. It looks like counting coins at midnight, eating rice and beans three nights straight, and patching shoes because new ones aren't an option. It doesn't feel brave. It doesn't look strong. But it is. It's survival disguised as ordinary life.

This stretch isn't about reacting in panic. It's about enduring the long middle, the part where every dollar is already spoken for. The crisis has passed, but the weight remains. Less chaos, more fatigue. Less sprinting, more trudging. Every act takes energy: stretching meals further than seems fair, juggling bills for one more delay, calling companies again and again for one more week. The weariness shows on your face, but so does the grit in your bones. That's what endurance looks like when falling turns into crawling.

The grind has no applause. No soundtrack, no speech, just quiet decisions no one sees. Cutting apples thinner so the kids don't notice there's less. Walking miles to save two dollars in bus fare. Pretending you're not hungry so the last serving goes to someone else. These aren't pity stories. They're proof of persistence. Each one whispers the same truth: you're still choosing to fight.

This isn't the place for luxury sacrifices or empty advice. No one here is debating lattes or vacations. This is about choices no one should have to make: food or gas, rent or heat, work phone or electricity. It's unfair, and it's nothing new. You've done smaller versions before: stretching leftovers, waiting for payday, surviving on fumes. But now, the stretch lasts longer. The waiting grows louder. What feels endless is still temporary even when the days blur.

There's no miracle coming. No lottery ticket. No secret fix. What comes next are tools: ways to eat when money is nearly gone, strategies to keep the lights on when funds are tight, and methods to earn quickly without falling into payday traps. This isn't theory. It's the muscle memory of survival.

Think of this part as motion after impact, not the crash, but the crawl. Scraped knees. Sleepless nights. Days that drain but still demand one more push. You're learning to stay afloat in a current that never stops pulling.

Reaching this point means you already have the strength most people never have to test. The next stretch will ask for more. It won't feel noble, but it will matter. Every coin stretched, every bill bargained, every meal pulled from scraps is proof of something greater: you haven't quit. You're still here. This is where survival shifts from chaos to endurance, and endurance, piece by piece, becomes the opening you've been fighting toward.

CHAPTER 6

BREAD AND BEANS — FOOD THAT FILLS FOR UNDER $2 A DAY

Hunger is the one bill you can't ignore. Rent can wait. Lights can flicker. But your stomach demands payment every single day. The good news? You can eat for under $2 a day. Forget fancy. Focus on full.

Staples That Stretch

Start with the cheapest fillers. Rice can feed a family for under two dollars a week. Pasta cooks quickly and pairs with nearly anything. Oats make dozens of bowls for pennies. Eggs remain one of the most affordable protein sources about thirty cents each. Pound for pound, potatoes fill you faster than almost anything else. Bread, beans, and peanut butter provide dense calories at low cost and keep you steady.

Angela once lived on rice, beans, and peanut butter for a full week on just six dollars' worth of food. Monotonous? Yes. Alive? Absolutely.

Don't overlook flour and tortillas. A single bag of flour can become flatbreads, dumplings, or pancakes. Tortillas turn beans, eggs, or vegetables into meals that feel bigger than they are. Malik bought a $3 bag of flour, added onions and beans, and fed his family of four for nearly two weeks.

Stretching the Basics.

Once the staples are covered, stretch them by adding inexpensive vegetables like onions, carrots, and cabbage to bulk up soups, stews, and stir-fries. Buying a whole chicken often costs less than buying its parts, and boiling the bones for broth creates multiple meals. Day-old bread becomes croutons or breadcrumbs. Leftover rice turns into fried rice.

Malik once spent a full month eating oats, potatoes, and cabbage, seasoning everything with broth cubes and oil. It wasn't balanced, but it was filling enough to carry him until payday.

Tonya learned to buy frozen vegetables instead of fresh ones. For five dollars, she stretched one bag across two weeks of stir-fries and soups. Her kids didn't care about presentation. They got vegetables daily, and that was enough.

Kids need calories more than variety. Oatmeal with a banana fills them for hours. Peanut butter sandwiches offer cheap protein. Rice with scrambled eggs makes a serviceable dinner. Angela made "survival pizza" using tortillas, tomato paste, and discounted cheese. It wasn't gourmet, but her kids smiled and ate. That was the victory.

No-Kitchen Survival

Not everyone has a stove. If you're living in a car, a shelter, or on a friend's couch, choose foods that can be eaten cold or made with just hot water. Bread, peanut butter, canned beans, tuna packets, apples, and bananas all work well. If you have a kettle or coffee maker, ramen noodles can be a lifesaver.

Jared spent three weeks living in his car, eating bread, peanut butter, canned chili, and bananas. He hated the monotony, but it kept him alive until he had a kitchen again.

Safety Note: Never use propane heaters or camp stoves indoors without ventilation. Carbon monoxide kills silently. Candles may seem cheap, but they can spark fires quickly. Cold meals are frustrating, but dangerous cooking methods can be deadly.

Community Resources

Food pantries and kitchens exist because millions have walked this same road. They aren't charity, they're strategy. Call 211 or check with local churches and nonprofits. Pantry boxes usually include beans, pasta, canned vegetables, and sometimes fresh produce. Janelle fed her kids for a week from one pantry box. It wasn't balanced, but her children ate breakfast every morning because she asked.

Many schools offer free or reduced breakfast and lunch. Some even run weekend "backpack programs" filled with snacks and staples. These programs are discreet; no child is singled out. If you have kids, this resource matters as much as rent or utilities.

Creative Fills

Beyond pantries, creativity stretches scraps. Popcorn kernels become days of snacks. Pancake mix doubles as bread. Instant potatoes thicken soups. Discounted yogurt near expiration makes a great breakfast addition.

David checked the clearance rack at his grocery store every night. He bought bruised fruit, dented cans, and nearly expired milk for pennies. His ten dollars stretched into nearly a week of meals. Always check dates and packaging. Buy only what you can use quickly. Cheap food wasted is money lost.

Hidden Helpers

Small tricks keep you going. A one-dollar spice jar can make plain rice more enjoyable. One bouillon cube turns water into soup. Salt, pepper, and garlic powder help combat flavor fatigue. Pre-portion meals to ensure everyone gets a fair share. Drink water often; it's free, filling, and helps ease hunger.

The Grind of Eating Broke

Eating like this isn't sustainable. It's not a healthy or nutritionally balanced long-term option. But in a crisis, it keeps you alive until income returns or help arrives. Use these strategies while job hunting, applying for aid, or waiting for your next check.

Broke meals aren't about pride, they're about persistence. Bread and beans, rice and potatoes, oats and eggs, they buy you time. And during a broke week, time means survival.

Angela's six-dollar week, Malik's month of cabbage, and David's clearance meals weren't pretty, but they kept households standing. Every pot of beans and peanut butter sandwich was proof that emptiness can be fought with grit and creativity.

Remember: the grind ends. Cheap meals aren't forever. They're the bridge between today's hunger and tomorrow's recovery. Every bowl, every portion, every stretch proves you're still fighting, and fighting means you're still here.

Emergency Moves

- **Buy staples cheaply:** rice, beans, pasta, oats, potatoes, eggs. Each dollar stretches for days.
- **Cook big, use small:** large pots of beans or rice can feed you in multiple ways.
- **Shop markdown racks**: dented cans, day-old bread, bruised produce, pennies for calories.
- **Swap smart:** popcorn instead of chips, water instead of soda, markdown meat over full price.
- **Stretch scraps:** stale bread into toast, rice into fried rice, beans into soup.
- **Tap resources:** pantries, schools, community kitchens. Asking isn't shameful; it's survival.

CHAPTER 7

THE CALL THAT CUTS YOUR BILL IN HALF — SCRIPTS THAT WORK

Bills arrive like verdicts, red stamps, glowing notifications, messages that feel final. They look carved in stone. But they're not. They're sand. Push, and they shift.

Companies don't lower bills out of kindness. They do it because keeping you is cheaper than losing you. That's your leverage. The moment you call, the balance of power shifts if you know what to say.

The Fear of the Call

Silence feels safer. Shame whispers that admitting you're short makes you weak. Maria believed that once. She stayed quiet, and her power was cut. The reconnection fee nearly doubled her balance. But next time, voice trembling, she called early. The representative offered a split-payment plan and ten extra days. Her balance shrank. Maria didn't get lucky. She pushed, and the wall moved.

James ignored his eviction notice. His landlord acted quickly, and court fees piled up. Silence cost him hundreds. The difference was simple: one stayed silent; the other made the call.

Words That Work

You don't need a speech. One line is enough:
"I want to pay, but I can't cover the full amount this week. What options do I have to avoid shutoff or fees?"

That sentence shifts you from avoidance to action. Derrick used it with his internet provider they cut $40 off his monthly bill for six months. Angela used it at a hospital billing office late fees vanished. One sentence saved them both money and time.

If the first person says no, don't stop. Ask for a supervisor. Call again at a different time, mid-morning or mid-week, often works best. Companies train staff differently; persistence reveals more options.

Beyond Utilities

Bills of all kinds can bend. Internet and phone providers may offer hardship programs or temporary discounts. Medical offices can reduce balances, waive late fees, or arrange zero-interest payment plans. Banks often reverse overdraft charges if you ask promptly and assertively. Even landlords might accept partial payments or grant short extensions, but always get agreements in writing. Verbal promises vanish; signed notes protect you.

The Silence After the Ask

Here's the hardest part: once you've asked, stop talking. Most people rush to fill the silence with apologies or excuses. Don't. Say your line, then pause. Representatives often need time to check systems, look up programs, or confirm what they can offer. In this moment, silence is strength.

The Psychology of Bills

Bills are designed to intimidate, to make you feel powerless. But every reduction, waived fee, and extension proves they can shift. Angela remembers hanging up after cutting her medical bill in half. She cried not just from relief, but from realizing the wall wasn't solid. It bent.

Each call proves you're still fighting. Every negotiation buys time to eat, keep the lights on, or make your next move. Bills aren't set in stone. They're sand. Push, and they shift.

Emergency Moves

- **Prepare**. Write down account numbers, balances, and what you can pay now.
- **Use the script** "I want to pay, but I can't cover the full amount this week. What options do I have to avoid shutoff or fees?"
- **Offer partial payments**. Even $20 or $30 shows effort and opens doors.
- **Hold the silence**. After asking, pause. Let them respond.
- **Challenge charges**. Request refunds for overdraft fees, late fees, or reconnection fees.
- **Get proof**. Always note names, dates, and confirmation numbers.
- **Stack small wins**. Cutting across multiple bills can free $100–$200 in a single week.

CHAPTER 8

LEAKY BUCKETS — STOPPING PAYDAY LOANS, OVERDRAFTS, AND TRAPS

You can hustle for cash and stretch every dollar, but it's worthless if your bucket keeps leaking. Payday loans, overdraft "protection," buy-now-pay-later schemes, and auto-pay withdrawals don't just drain money; they drain your time, effort, and stability. What looks like a lifeline is often just another hole.

These four traps target people in crisis. Payday loans exploit panic. Overdraft fees punish bad timing. BNPL lures you in with convenience, then locks you in. Auto-pay strips away control. Each one stings. Together, they keep you broke.

Payday Loans Triple the Cost

Payday loans advertise speed: fast cash, no questions asked. But the cost is brutal. Borrow $300 and roll it over once or twice, and you could end up repaying $900. More than 80% of payday loans are re-borrowed within two weeks. That cycle isn't a mistake; it's the business model.

Marcus learned that the hard way. A loan to cover rent led to another to cover the first. Within three months, half his paycheck was gone before he even saw it. The loan didn't save him; it sold him time at triple the cost.

Fix: Call the lender and ask about extended payment plans. Many states require them by law. Check with credit unions or nonprofits for small-dollar loans at humane rates. Even $100 from a friend or local aid group costs less than the payday trap.

Overdraft "Protection" Banks Selling You Your Own Money

Banks market overdraft as safety. It's not. It's a $35 penalty for buying groceries with $5 in your account. Three small charges in one day, and $15 in food becomes $120 in fees.

Angela watched $200 vanish into overdrafts in two weeks. Her balance wasn't feeding her kids; it was feeding the bank.

Fix: Opt out of overdraft "protection." If you're charged, call within 24 hours. Many banks will refund at least one fee if you ask quickly. Stick to cash or prepaid cards. Better a declined charge than another $35 penalty.

Buy Now, Pay Later Debt Hidden as Convenience

BNPL makes debt look harmless. Four small payments. No interest until you miss one. Then come the fees, then the collectors. Companies like Klarna, Afterpay, and Affirm thrive because tomorrow's paycheck always feels safer than today's reality.

Derrick bought a $400 console this way. Late payments and penalties pushed the total to $600. What felt like freedom became a trap with receipts.

Fix: Avoid BNPL unless it's a true emergency, and you're certain you can cover. Already caught in one? Contact the company before default. Many will reschedule if you reach out early.

Auto-Pay Convenience That Comes First

Auto-pay feels safe because bills are handled automatically. But when money's tight, it becomes a trigger. Rosa's gas bill cleared the day before payday. Overdraft fees wiped out her grocery budget. Convenience turned into a crisis.

Fix: Turn off auto-pay for anything nonessential. Pay manually so you control when money leaves. You're not dodging bills, you're managing timing.

Patching the Leaks

None of these traps is an accident. They're engineered to profit from panic. But leaks can be sealed. Cancel overdraft "protection." Refuse payday loans. Resist BNPL. Switch off auto-pay. Each repair keeps money in your hands instead of theirs.

And once the leaks slow, build a tiny buffer. Even $20 matters. It's one grocery trip that doesn't overdraft, one bus fare that doesn't trigger panic, one meal that doesn't require borrowing. Malik built his cushion with coins from his car, a weekend delivery shift, and selling clothes. The $28 he saved didn't erase his bills, but it kept his account positive when auto-pay tried to pull. That margin stopped another spiral.

Fixing leaks isn't glamorous. It's not instant. But once the bucket holds water, every dollar you hustle finally counts. And when it does, the next step isn't just patching holes, it's filling faster. That's where we go next.

Every meal you've built from almost nothing is a declaration: *I refuse to disappear.* You've cooked dignity out of scarcity, turned hunger into motion, and kept love alive on borrowed strength. These small acts don't make you weak; they make you unbreakable. Bread and beans fed your body, but persistence fed your soul.

CHAPTER 9

THE RENT WALL: WHAT TO DO WHEN SHELTER IS AT RISK

Groceries can stretch. Bills can bend. Lights can wait. But shelter feels immovable. Rent isn't just another bill; it's a wall: tall, heavy, and ready to collapse if you miss. When money doesn't match the demand, fear hits harder than hunger because homelessness feels final.

Silence Versus Action

Maria once ignored her landlord, hoping to stall until payday. Silence cost her court fees and an eviction record that followed her for years. Angela faced the same shortfall but made a call within 24 hours. She explained, offered a partial payment, and asked for options. The landlord granted a two-week extension. Same crisis, two outcomes. The difference? Angela picked up the phone.

Landlords don't lower rent out of kindness, but communication can shift how they see you. Hiding makes you seem risky. Speaking up even with $50 on a $500 balance shows you're trying. A tenant who communicates appears safer than one who vanishes.

Here's a script:
"I want to pay, but I can't cover the full amount this week. What options do I have to avoid eviction or late fees?"

It doesn't guarantee success, but it changes the tone. Every day of silence weakens your footing. Every call buys breathing room.

When the Law Creates Space

Sometimes the wall holds firm, but the law forces patience. Many states require grace periods before eviction can proceed. Some mandate mediation or payment plans. In California, for example, eviction proceedings typically take at least 30 days from the first notice. That's time to maneuver.

Contact 211, Legal Aid, or HUD housing counselors to understand your rights. Don't guess laws vary by state and city. A ten-minute call can uncover protections that buy you time. Knowledge doesn't erase rent, but it delays consequences. And delay can mean the difference between keeping your home and scrambling for shelter.

Cracks in the Wall Creative Alternatives

When negotiation and law can't carry you further, look for cracks in the wall. Some landlords accept labor instead of money: painting, yard work, or maintenance. Others may allow subletting or adding a roommate. Downsizing to a smaller unit, moving in with family, or renting out storage space are imperfect but workable strategies. None erases rent, but each creates a foothold.

David avoided eviction by renting his spare room for $250 a month. Rosa babysat for her landlord's family, which reduced her balance for three months. Malik took on yard work that earned him a $100 credit. These weren't forever solutions. They were rungs on a ladder enough to climb another day.

Preparing for the Worst

Sometimes the wall doesn't move. When eviction is imminent, preparation becomes survival. Track every payment, email, and conversation. Use free apps like Google Drive or Evernote to store records in case of court. Quietly pack essentials: IDs, medications, school records, and a small emergency kit. Protect your security deposit by documenting your unit's condition with photos and video before leaving. That money is yours, don't let it vanish.

If eviction is unavoidable, minimize the damage:

- Ask your landlord about a "cash for keys" deal, leaving quickly in exchange for debt forgiveness.
- Request a reference letter, even after default.
- Contact nonprofits, churches, or mutual aid groups for temporary housing.
- Treat shelters as a last resort, but bring documentation to speed rehousing.

Prevention Before the Wall

The best way to avoid hitting the wall is to reroute before you reach it. If rent swallows most of your paycheck, consider adding a roommate, moving to a smaller unit, or relocating closer to work to save on transportation. Cash advance apps or emergency loans from credit unions aren't ideal, but they can cover a one-week gap and help you avoid the far higher cost of eviction fees and records.

Above all, make rent your top priority. Other bills can bend later. Housing is the foundation everything else rests.

The Weight and the Climb

The rent wall is heavy but not solid. Every call, partial payment, and creative choice is a crack that lets light through. Fear hits hardest here, but paralysis guarantees eviction. Action, even if imperfect, buys you room to climb.

This isn't the end of your story. Even if you lose one place, you can rebuild. Deposits can be restored. Shelters are temporary. Records fade. What matters is refusing to stop moving. Each foothold, no matter how small, proves you can climb again.

Emergency Moves

- Call your landlord within 24 hours; silence closes doors.
- Make partial payments, even $40 shows effort.
- Document agreements, email, text, or signed notes to protect you.
- Contact 211, Legal Aid, or HUD for rental assistance and tenant rights.
- Review state grace periods and mediation rules.
- Explore work-for-rent, roommates, or subletting if allowed.
- Prepare essentials if eviction is imminent: IDs, meds, records, safe shelter.
- Request your security deposit in writing; it's your money.

CHAPTER 10

WHEELS ON FUMES — SURVIVING TRANSPORTATION WITHOUT CASH

No wheels, no work. No work, no income. That's why losing gas money, bus fare, or a working car isn't just an inconvenience; it's lost wages. Transportation is the link that holds survival together. Without it, paychecks don't arrive, groceries can't be carried home, and overdue bills multiply.

Tonya learned this when her car's transmission failed. The repair cost was $1,200, but her paycheck was $900. She could have borrowed, but debt would have buried her. Instead, she bought a used bike for $40. She hated riding in the rain, hated sore legs, hated showing up to work damp and tired. But she never missed a shift. The bike didn't solve everything, but it kept income flowing. In broke weeks, that's the only math that matters.

Stretching the Tank You Have

If you've still got a quarter tank, think in days, not miles. A quarter tank can last three to four days if you cut trips to essentials only. Carpool to work, batch errands, and skip every unnecessary drive. Drive slower, keep your tires inflated, and don't idle. Every mile you save is another mile toward your next paycheck.

Apps like GasBuddy or Waze help you find the cheapest stations. Loyalty programs at Kroger, Shell, Exxon, or Costco can save 10 to 20 cents per gallon. That difference stretches the last $10 in your pocket into two more days of commuting.

Malik turned one tank into nine days. He parked two miles from work and walked the rest, nearly halving his driving. His coworkers teased him, but those nine days gave him the time he needed until payday. It wasn't convenient. It wasn't easy. But it kept his job secure.

Creative Fills and Quick Fixes

When the tank runs dry, look for alternatives. Many transit agencies offer hardship passes, reduced-fare programs, or emergency ride vouchers, often buried deep on their websites. Call 211 to ask about bus tokens or gas cards. Churches and nonprofits sometimes keep them on hand for exactly this reason.

If cash is gone, barter. Yard work for gas. Babysitting for rides. Cleaning for bus money. In Chicago, one man cleaned his mechanic's garage in exchange for two weeks of rides. Awkward? Yes. But it worked. When dollars run out, labor becomes your currency.

David faced this choice when his car died. The repair estimate was higher than the car's value. He bought a $70 bike on Facebook Marketplace and added a $12 headlight and lock from a thrift store. That bike carried him six miles each way for months. It wasn't safe in every storm, but it kept him employed. If biking becomes your lifeline, invest in the basics: lights, a helmet, and a secure lock. A stolen bike during a broke week is a second crisis.

Surviving Without Wheels

Sometimes, the car is gone for good. That's when the world shrinks. But smaller doesn't mean no movement; it means finding new patterns. Ask your employer about compressed schedules, four long days instead of five shorter ones, to cut commuting costs by 20%. Some jobs may allow limited remote work if you frame it as a survival need.

Build a carpool network before the crisis hits. Coworkers, neighbors, or church members are often open to sharing rides if you cover gas, swap chores, or cook meals in return. Explore community bike-share programs or nonprofit bike libraries. They may not advertise widely, but they exist in many cities.

Sometimes survival means relocating closer to work or transit. Downsizing to a smaller apartment can reduce both rent and transportation costs. Janelle survived two weeks without gas by walking her kids to school and catching rides from a coworker three days a week. She was exhausted, but she kept her paycheck. And that paycheck kept her home.

The Fear Factor

Transportation failure carries its own weight. Losing lights hurts. Losing food hurts. But losing movement feels like the world closing in. Routes shrink. Choices shrink. Freedom shrinks. But shrinking isn't stopping.

Every mile walked, every bus token scraped, every ride bartered is proof the world hasn't ended, it's just smaller for now. And small still gets you through the door to work.

Emergency Moves

- **Stretch what you have.** Batch errands, inflate tires, slow down, and cut all unnecessary trips.
- **Find discounted fuel.** Use GasBuddy, loyalty cards, and grocery programs for cheaper gas.
- **Seek local aid**: Call 211, ask nonprofits or churches for bus tokens or gas cards.
- **Barter rides** offer babysitting, yard work, or cleaning in exchange for transportation.
- **Secure a bike.** Check thrift stores, Facebook Marketplace, or nonprofit bike programs; always add lights, a helmet, and a lock.
- **Carpool smart.** Build ride networks with coworkers or neighbors.
- **Negotiate schedules.** Ask about compressed weeks or remote shifts.
- **Protect insurance.** Call providers before missing payments; hardship options exist.
- **Calculate repairs first.** Don't sink money into a car worth less than the fix.

CHAPTER 11

COLD NIGHTS, DARK ROOMS — SURVIVING UTILITIES WHEN THEY'RE CUT OFF

Cold nights teach you something heat never could: how to keep moving when comfort disappears. You've learned that power isn't just electricity, it's resolve. The lights may go out, but the will to keep trying doesn't. Every blanket, every borrowed shower, every glow stick that makes a child smile is proof that you can still create warmth in the dark. This isn't a weakness. It's the kind of strength only hardship reveals.

Step One: Call Fast

Don't wait a day. Don't wait an hour. Call within a few hours of shutoff, even if it feels humiliating. Companies often offer hardship programs, payment plans, or emergency grants, but you must request them promptly.

Angela ignored a $200 bill until her power was cut. Embarrassment burned hotter than her cold apartment. When she finally called, the agent offered to restore service for $50 upfront and let her pay the rest over time. That call didn't erase her debt, but it gave her back heat and breathing room.

Utility reps vary in discretion. Some will say no. Others will look harder. If the first shuts you down, ask for a supervisor or call again later.

Script: "I want to pay, but I can't cover the full amount today. What's the minimum to avoid reconnection fees?"

Ten minutes can change your week.

Many states legally require utilities to offer payment plans or protections during extreme weather. Contact your state's public utility commission or Legal Aid to learn what applies where you live. Knowledge doesn't wipe out the bill, but it buys you time. And time is leverage.

Step Two: Adapt When the Lights Stay Out

If reconnection isn't possible right away, shift from negotiating to adapting. The goal: stay warm, fed, and functional until service returns.

Heat: Layer clothes, sleep in one room, and use blankets or sleeping bags. Borrow or rent a safe space heater, but ventilate properly. Never use ovens, grills, or camp stoves indoors. Carbon monoxide is silent and deadly. Even a few tealight candles under a ceramic pot can radiate warmth in a small space, but use extreme caution and never leave them unattended.

Light: Solar garden lights charge during the day and shine at night. Glow sticks are safe for children. Candles work, but fire is a real risk. Keep water nearby and never sleep with a flame burning. During one blackout, Malik's kids used glow sticks to play cards. It wasn't comfort, but it reminded them they weren't powerless.

Water: Fill every container, jug, bottle, and pot before the shutoff. Jared once filled 14 bottles, and they lasted a week for cooking, hygiene, and drinking. If your area has public water fountains, refill discreetly.

Cooking: A camping stove works if used outside or in a ventilated space. Angela borrowed one from a neighbor and cooked noodles on the balcony.

Awkward? Yes. Effective? Absolutely. Backyard grills can also boil water or heat soup when other options run out.

Step Three: Rely on Your Community

Utility poverty is common. Assistance exists because millions face it. Call 211, the national hotline for local resources. Ask about LIHEAP (Low-Income Home Energy Assistance Program), the Salvation Army, Catholic Charities, or local nonprofits. Many offer vouchers or direct aid.

Malik kept quiet for a week while his apartment stayed dark. Shame nearly swallowed him. When he finally admitted it to a friend, they connected him to a church fund that paid half his bill. Asking felt humiliating. Staying silent was worse.

Neighbors can help too. Borrow a shower, charge a phone, share a hot meal. It may sting to ask, but those small favors keep you going until reconnection.

The Mental Weight

Utility shutoffs don't just freeze your room; they freeze your mind. Embarrassment feels heavier than cold. You imagine everyone knows. You think you've failed. But here's the truth: millions have been here, and most get through by asking questions, adapting, and holding on. Using glow sticks or eating cold beans doesn't mean failure; it means you're still in the fight.

Emergency Moves

- **Call immediately**. Ask about hardship programs, payment plans, or minimum reinstatement amounts.
- **Check protections**. Review your state's utility shutoff laws with the public utility commission.

- **Adapt safely**. Layer clothes, limit to one room, and never use stoves or grills indoors.
- **Light smart**ly. Use solar lights, glow sticks, or candles only with caution.
- **Stock water**: Fill jugs and bottles before cutoff; refill when possible.
- **Seek help**: Call 211, LIHEAP, the Salvation Army, or local churches for aid.
- **Plan for reconnection**. Most services return within 24–72 hours after payment. Prepare food, light, and warmth to bridge the gap.

Part III

THE HUMAN WEIGHT

You've reached the point where survival no longer means just finding food or paying bills. You've kept the lights on, stretched the rice, and bargained through another month, but now the weight has moved inward. The hardest part isn't what's in your wallet; it's what the fight has done to your spirit. This part isn't about math or budgeting. It's about the cost of carrying constant pressure and how to protect the parts of you that money can't replace. You're not rebuilding finances yet. You're rebuilding yourself.

When Money Becomes More Than Math

Money problems aren't just math; they're pressure. You feel them in your chest when sleep won't come, in your shoulders when you walk into work, and in the silence when your kids ask for something you can't give. They're not just numbers on a bill; they're burdens you carry everywhere.

That weight doesn't vanish when rent is scraped together or another bill is patched. It lingers. It follows you into conversations, into the way you eat, into how you love and how you fight. Stress becomes a second job that never clocks out. And some days, it feels heavier than the bills themselves.

The Hidden Costs You Carry

The costs are invisible but real. Panic attacks that mimic heart failure. Shame that keeps you from making a call. Anger that spills onto the people you love. Isolation that convinces you you're alone when you're not. The mask you wear daily so the world won't see the cracks. You can adjust the numbers, but if you overlook this part, stress will find other ways to surface.

What This Section Is About

This isn't about coins or coupons. It's about the toll of constant scrambling on your mind, body, relationships, and spirit. Poverty isn't just an empty wallet. It's the exhaustion of carrying that emptiness everywhere you go.

Endurance Beyond the Numbers

The same grit that stretched rice and bargained bills is the grit needed here. Endurance isn't just financial, it's emotional. It's learning how to silence shame before it crushes you, how to hold your family together when money tries to pull it apart, and how to protect your mind so it doesn't break while you're fixing everything else.

Where We Go From Here

From here, we turn to the hidden battles. We'll begin with stress and its effects on the body, then confront shame, the silent poison that convinces you you're less than others. We'll examine the damage financial strain inflicts on relationships and how to protect the people you love from that fallout. Finally, we'll face the toll on your mind, fear, despair, and the lies that whisper you can't keep going.

This won't be easy reading. But neither is living through it. Still, if you've made it this far, you've already proven something debt doesn't want you to know: its story about you is wrong. You're stronger than the burden you've been carrying. Strong enough not just to endure the grind but to push through it without letting the weight break you.

The bills are visible. The effort is apparent. But the unseen burden, the one in your chest, your head, your home, is just as real. That's what this section is about: identifying it, understanding it, and learning to bear it until stability returns.

CHAPTER 12

SHAME IS A DEBT YOU DON'T OWE — BREAKING THE SILENCE

Shame is the bill no one sends, but everyone pays. It doesn't arrive in an envelope, but it drains you faster than late fees. It has no due date, yet it shows up whenever you consider asking for help. Shame whispers you're weak. It convinces you to hide. And hiding costs more than any overdue notice.

Angela learned this lesson when she fell behind on her light bill. Embarrassment kept her from calling. She told herself she'd figure it out alone. By the time she reached out, the power was already cut, and the reconnection fee doubled her debt. Shame didn't just silence her; it emptied her pockets.

Malik faced the same shortfall. His gas bill was due, and he only had part of the money. He swallowed his pride, picked up the phone, and said, "I want to pay, but I can't cover the full amount this week. What options do I have to avoid shutoff?" Ten minutes later, he had an extension and a split payment plan. The difference wasn't luck; it was timing. Malik acted before silence closed his options.

Tonya's story shows how shame grows heavier with larger bills. She was hit with a $1,200 hospital charge she didn't expect. Shame told her not to question it. She almost signed up for a high-interest credit card just to cover the balance. Instead, a friend urged her to call the hospital's billing office. She asked about hardship programs. The bill dropped to $400 with a six-month plan. The help had always been available. Silence nearly buried her in debt.

That's what shame does. It doesn't just weigh on you; it blocks action. It stops you from dialing the number, opening the letter, or talking to the person who could help. Silence feels safe, but it's a trap. Hiding guarantees nothing will change. Speaking up opens doors.

Breaking the Silence

The first step is choosing your audience. Not everyone has the authority to act. Receptionists rarely approve extensions, but billing supervisors, property managers, and hardship teams can. Aim for decision-makers. Keep it brief, confident, and early. The first call matters most within hours of a shutoff notice, not days later.

Here are three scripts that work:

- **Utility bill:** "I want to pay, but I can't cover the full amount this week. What options do I have to keep service on?"
- **Landlord:** "I can't pay the full rent today, but I can pay [amount] now and the rest by [date]. Can we put this in writing?"
- **Medical provider:** "I want to pay, but this bill is beyond my means. Do you have hardship reductions or payment plans?"

Each script is short. No excuses. No speeches. Just facts and effort. Then stop. The silence after your request feels unbearable, but that pause is where decisions get made. Don't rush to fill it. Wait for their answer.

Handling Rejection

Not every call succeeds. Sometimes you'll hear, "We can't do that." That isn't the end. Call back later. Ask for a supervisor. Try again another day. Policies change with the person, the time of day, and your persistence. Different voice, different outcome.

Shame thrives on rejection, convincing you it's proof you shouldn't have tried. But the truth is the opposite: every attempt proves you're still fighting. Each call, whether it ends with yes or no, keeps options alive.

Replacing Shame with Connection

Shame isolates. Connection multiplies. Friends, neighbors, churches, nonprofits, these networks exist because millions have walked the same road. Choose allies carefully. Trust those who listen without judgment and offer real solutions. Avoid people who turn your struggle into gossip or blame.

Angela eventually admitted her situation to a neighbor who had been through the same thing. That neighbor pointed her to a church utility fund. The $75 she received kept her lights on another week. The help was always nearby, but silence had kept her from seeing it.

The Real Debt

The real debt isn't shame. It's the overdue bill, the dark apartment, the landlord's notice. Shame convinces you to pay it first, but shame isn't owed. Survival is. Every word you speak, every request you make, chips away at that false balance. Pride may bruise. But bruises heal. Shutoffs don't.

You don't owe silence. You don't owe shame. You owe your future. Speak.

Emergency Moves

- **Call early** within hours of a shutoff or notice, not after fees multiply.
- **Target decision-makers**, supervisors, property managers, hardship teams, not receptionists.
- **Use proven scripts** to keep asks short, clear, and focused on options to prevent shutoff or eviction.
- **Handle rejection** call back, request a supervisor, or try a different day or agent.
- **Choose trustworthy allies** who confide only in people who offer solutions instead of adding shame.

CHAPTER 13

THE HIDDEN HANDS — CHURCHES, CHARITIES, AND MUTUAL AID

There are hands out there you can't see. They don't appear on your bills or in your banking app. They exist quietly in neighborhoods, faith communities, and living rooms, hands that catch people when the system lets them fall. These hands don't erase every problem, but they can lighten the weight just enough to keep you moving. Using them doesn't make you weak. It makes you resourceful.

What's Actually Available

Churches, charities, and mutual aid networks each play different roles. Churches often move the fastest gas cards, food boxes, and even emergency utility payments through benevolence funds. Charities like the Salvation Army, Catholic Charities, or United Way run more structured programs. They may cover rent or bills, but usually require paperwork. Mutual aid groups work differently. They're neighbors pooling funds through Facebook, WhatsApp, or community boards. They don't follow strict rules and often respond quickly because it's personal.

Timing matters. Churches may help the same day. Charities are best early in the month before funds run out. Mutual aid is less predictable but often faster than official programs. Knowing when to reach out isn't luck, it's strategy.

Documentation and Procedures

Most organizations don't demand a mountain of forms. Basics like an ID, proof of address, or a past-due notice are often enough. If you're missing something, ask what alternatives they'll accept. A landlord's note, a bill screenshot, or a pay stub might suffice. Angela once delayed applying because she thought she needed tax returns. In the end, her overdue light bill was accepted as proof. She left with a $50 grocery card.

Delays happen. Rosa applied for rent assistance through a charity but was told the check would take three weeks. Her landlord couldn't wait. A local mutual aid group raised $150 in two days. It wasn't the full rent, but it bought her enough time for the charity's payment to arrive.

Breaking Through the Barriers

The most challenging obstacle isn't paperwork; it's silence. Pride says Don't ask. Fear says they'll judge you. But silence guarantees nothing. A simple script works: "I'm behind on rent [or lights, or food]. Do you have assistance programs?" Those words don't need polish; they need to be said.

Direct your request to the right person. Receptionists can't approve extensions. Supervisors, outreach directors, or coordinators can. Too often, "We can't help" really means "I can't approve this." Ask for someone with authority.

Expect rejection. Sometimes funds are gone. Sometimes the answer is "Try again next month." Painful, yes, but one "no" isn't final. Malik contacted three churches before one said yes. That one, yes, kept his lights on.

The Real Value

Cash helps, but goods matter too. Groceries, diapers, transit cards, or utility vouchers save money you'd otherwise spend. Taking them isn't charity, it's strategy. Every food box frees up cash for rent. Every gas card stretches your paycheck.

And beyond dollars and goods, there's solidarity. Mutual aid, especially, shows that survival isn't just about grit; it's about community. Strangers step in where systems fail, proving you're not fighting alone. The hidden hands are proof that resilience is a shared, not solitary, experience.

Debt can count dollars, but it can't measure you. You've walked through fear and still found the strength to seek out the light. You've learned that survival isn't about luck, it's about returning to yourself after the world has tried to price your worth. You are not a story of shortage. You are a story of resilience becoming wisdom.

CHAPTER 14

ALONE AT THE TABLE — SURVIVING THE MENTAL CRASH

You sit at the table, bills stacked in front of you, the fridge humming, or maybe it's dark. The weight isn't just numbers anymore. It's the hollow in your stomach, the ache in your chest, the exhaustion that seeps into your bones. This is the mental crash. It isn't just about unpaid bills. It's the moment survival shifts from money to willpower.

When the Crash Hits

The crash creeps in after too many days of strain. It sounds like silence is a signal of defeat. It feels like heavy pressure when you think about dialing the phone or opening another letter. It shows up in your body: sleepless nights, missed meals, headaches, shallow breathing, stomach knots, and fatigue so deep it feels like wading through mud.

It whispers lies: You're failing. You're alone. There's no way forward. It convinces you that asking for help is pointless and that tomorrow will bring the same rejection. That's the trap. Quiet turns into paralysis, and paralysis makes bills, hunger, and fear multiply.

Proof in People

Angela hit her breaking point when her lights went out. Shame told her not to call, but hours later, desperation pushed her to act. She explained she could pay $50 on her $200 balance. The agent granted her an extension. One small step restored heat and bought her three days of breathing room.

Marcus heard the same voices but stayed silent. He waited for payday. By the weekend, his utilities had been shut off, and reconnecting them would cost him triple. His inaction turned a struggle into a disaster. The difference wasn't luck; it was action.

Others broke the spiral in smaller ways. Janelle couldn't bring herself to make a call, but she cleaned her kitchen, ate a slice of bread, and wrote one bill on a piece of paper. That tiny act gave her a sense of control. Sometimes, the smallest steps can prevent the crash from consuming you.

Breaking the Spiral

The crash isn't a failure; it's exhaustion from fighting too long without relief. The first step is to name it. Say out loud: *This is the crash. It's not me. It's the pressure talking.* Naming separates the burden from your identity.

Next, act not with grand gestures, but with one small move. Make a call. Pay $10. Write a single email. Step outside for fresh air. Even a short action breaks paralysis and proves momentum is possible.

Then, connect. Call a friend, a sibling, or a hotline for support. Hearing another human voice say, "*We can help,*" can tip the balance. If speaking feels impossible, send a text. Silence feeds despair; connection interrupts it.

Finally, rest. Rest isn't quitting, it's fuel. Sleep for two hours, drink water, and eat something with protein. Many crashes intensify because exhaustion takes over. Recharging isn't a weakness; it's preparation for the next move.

The Hidden Cost

Mental crashes don't just weigh on you; they ripple outward. Partners notice the quiet. Children sense the tension. Friends pick up on withdrawal. You don't need to share every detail, but you can say, *"I'm struggling today." "I need quiet,"* or *"I need help with dinner."* That honesty replaces isolation with support.

Children, in particular, notice more than parents think. For younger children, simple reassurance is often enough: *"Money is tight, but we're safe."* Older kids may need honesty with limits: *"I'm working on paying bills. It's stressful, but I'll handle it."* Teens often want to help give them age-appropriate ways to pitch in without making them carry the full weight.

How Long Does It Last

Crashes pass. Most fade within hours or days once small actions and rest interrupt the spiral. If a crash lingers longer than a week, or if hopeless thoughts become dangerous, reach out for professional help. In the U.S., dial 988 for the Suicide & Crisis Lifeline. In other countries, search for your local hotline and save the number for later. Preparation is also survival.

Emergency Moves

- **Name it**. Say aloud: *"This is the crash. It's not me."* Naming separates you from the burden.
- **Do one thing**: Make a call, send an email, write one bill, or eat a small meal. Action breaks paralysis.

- **Find a micro-win**. Clean a corner, pay $5, take a short walk. Wins stack into progress.
- **Rest and refuel**. Sleep, hydrate, and eat protein. Crashes worsen when your body is empty.
- **Reach out** Contact friends, family, hotlines, or support groups. Replace silence with connection.
- **Plan tomorrow**. Write one small, specific action for the next day. Keep it achievable.

A crash isn't proof you're broken. It's proof you've been carrying too much for too long. The table, the bills, the silence, none of these define you. What defines you is getting back up, one small act at a time.

CHAPTER 15

HUNGRY CHILDREN, HEAVY HEARTS —HOLDING THE FAMILY TOGETHER

When children look up at you with hungry eyes, the burden feels heavier than any bill. Rent notices and overdue balances weigh you down, but nothing compares to an empty plate in front of your child. That moment cuts deeper than the fear of eviction or losing electricity. It feels personal, as if poverty has invaded your kitchen and stolen your dignity.

Hunger is relentless because it's visible. You can hide unpaid bills. You can silence a phone demanding money. But you can't silence the sound of a stomach growling across the table. Parents fear not only that their children will feel hunger but that they will remember it forever. That fear is sharp, but the truth is gentler: children remember not the size of the meals, but how you carried them through the hard seasons.

Feeding on Almost Nothing

Parents under pressure get creative. Bread becomes "survival pizza" with sauce packets. Instant noodles stretch into soup for three when bulked with an egg and frozen vegetables. Candlelight, meant to mask a power cut, is reframed as "family night." Marcus once spread a blanket on the floor and called it a picnic. His children laughed more that night than in weeks. Rosa sliced bread into tiny squares and called them "mini-sandwiches." Her kids treated them as a game, not a loss. These small reframes don't erase hunger, but they soften its edge and remind children they're loved.

School resources often go untapped. Many districts offer free or reduced-price breakfasts and lunches, weekend backpack programs, and after-school snacks. Asking doesn't label your children; it protects them. Teachers and school counselors can connect you quietly. For single parents, these programs often become the difference between despair and perseverance.

Talking to Children Without Breaking Them

What you say matters, but so does what you leave unsaid. Explaining too much burdens children; saying nothing leaves them anxious. Honest, age-appropriate language protects both truth and hope. Toddlers need reassurance more than facts: *"Daddy's working on grocery money."* School-age children can absorb simple truths: *"Money is tight, but we're safe."* Teens need partnership: *"We're struggling this month. If you have ideas, I'm listening."*

Naming stress without blame keeps bonds intact. Instead of snapping, *"We don't have enough because of you,"* try: *"We're scared, and we're tired, but we're a team."* Children may forget the words, but they'll remember whether home felt safe, even when meals were small.

Holding Families Together During Tough Times

Hunger doesn't just strain parents and kids; it strains couples. Arguments about bills often mask deeper fears: of failing, of losing security, of not being enough. Couples who survive aren't the ones with perfect answers; they're the ones who refuse to turn on each other when the pressure peaks.

For single parents, the burden doubles. You become both provider and comforter. Rituals become survival tools: bedtime stories even in the dark, games while waiting at food banks, or a "special meal" like Sunday pancakes, even if thinner than usual. Rituals remind children that we are still ourselves.

An extended family can help too. Grandparents watching kids while you work, siblings pooling groceries, or cousins carpooling to school all lighten the load. Don't underestimate how even a few hours of relief can steady a household under strain.

What Children Remember

Hunger passes. Lights return. Rent gets paid. What remains are memories of how you showed up when everything felt fragile. Children remember your voice, turning scarcity into story. They remember your arms around them when the world felt unstable. They remember the effort to shield them from shame. They won't recall the number of noodles in the pot. They'll recall who sat beside them while they ate.

Heavy hearts can still be steady ones. What defines these moments isn't how much food was on the table; it's whether love stayed present when resources vanished.

Emergency Moves

- **Use school programs**: Apply for free/reduced lunches, weekend food packs, and after-school snacks. Quiet, practical, immediate.
- **Make simple meals:** Rice with beans, bread with sauce, oats with fruit. Calories first, variety later.

- **Reframe scarcity:** Call outages "family nights," floor dinners, "picnics," simple meals, "special recipes." Framing shields children from despair.
- **Talk at their level.** Toddlers need reassurance, kids need simple honesty, and teens need partnership. Always speak without shame.
- **Stay united** with a partner, fight the bills, not each other. As a single parent, anchor routines and rituals.
- **Ask early.** Food banks, pantries, churches, and schools provide meals quickly. Goods matter as much as cash.

CHAPTER 16

THE NEIGHBOR'S KNOCK — ASKING FOR HELP WITHOUT LOSING YOURSELF

Pride is quiet until the knock comes. It's the moment you hear yourself saying, *"I'm fine,"* when you're not. It's pretending the lights are on when the house is dark, smiling so no one sees the cracks. Still, there comes a point when silence grows too heavy to hold. Sometimes, survival begins with the knock you've been avoiding, your hand raised, your voice small, your need spoken aloud.

You learn that not knowing doesn't always mean being lost; sometimes, it means being still long enough to let life find its rhythm again.

Asking for help feels like surrender. You fear judgment, pity, and rejection. The world teaches that strength means silence, that independence equals dignity. But that lesson is a lie designed to keep people struggling alone. The truth is simple: asking is not weakness; it's wisdom. It means knowing your worth isn't measured by what you carry alone, but by what you're brave enough to share.

When Pride Blocks the Door

Angela learned that truth one winter night. Her heat was cut off, her children wrapped in coats beneath blankets. She had twenty dollars to her name and no plan. The next morning, she knocked on her neighbor Rosa's door. Rosa didn't judge. She listened. Within an hour, Angela's family had hot soup, extra blankets, and a contact for a church fund that paid half her bill. What began as shame became rescue.

Later, Angela admitted the hardest part wasn't asking, it was realizing how long she had suffered trying not to. That moment changed her. She began leaving small kindnesses for others: extra mittens on a porch, a bag of groceries with no note, envelopes with five-dollar bills tucked beneath a mat. Each act whispered, *"I remember."* The courage to ask had become the courage to give.

The First Ask

Help is not only about a crisis. Sometimes, it's about easing the weight of exhaustion before it crushes you. In the weeks that followed, Angela noticed how differently she saw the world. She began to recognize quiet signs: the porch light that stayed off too long, the sound of a zipper scraping the cold, the half-smile of someone pretending they were fine. Before, she would have looked away, afraid to intrude. Now, she stepped forward. That's what asking does. It rewires empathy. Once you've had to knock, you never ignore another door.

Help doesn't always mean handouts. Sometimes, it's shared tools, rides, meals, or simply the name of someone who knows someone. The key is intention. You're not begging; you're bridging. You're saying, *"I'm doing everything I can. I just need one more step to get through this week."* That sentence turns pity into partnership. The moment you ask, you give another person's compassion a place to live. You remind them that giving is not charity, it's a connection.

Finding the Right Ears

When you reach out, choose wisely. Not every ear deserves your truth. Some people listen for gossip, not to help. Look for those who have struggled who speak with empathy rather than offering advice. People who have been broke know the sound of desperation. They recognize it; they don't judge it. Ask them first. They'll answer differently. They'll say, *"I've been there,"* instead of *"You should have."* That difference matters. It's the line between being seen and being studied.

Keep your boundaries clear. Accept what helps you stand, not what makes you shrink. If someone tries to trade help for control, walk away. Real aid doesn't demand your silence, your debt, or your humiliation. Real help is light shared, not light stolen. It often comes wrapped in imperfection, maybe late, maybe small, maybe awkward, yet offered with sincerity. Accept that. Grace usually looks like an inconvenience wrapped in kindness.

Turning Help into Habit

When you're back on your feet, knock on someone else's door. Pay forward what pride once kept you from receiving. A man named Marcus learned this after losing his job of twenty years. For months, he walked past the same community center offering free meals, too proud to step inside. The day he finally did, a volunteer greeted him by name, someone who remembered when Marcus coached the neighborhood kids. That one act of recognition melted his shame. He didn't just eat that day; he exhaled.

The next week, he returned to sweep the floors. Two months later, after finding steady work, he came back every Saturday to serve others. He never forgot that one simple plate of food restored his dignity. The cycle completes when help becomes a habit, when the knock you once dreaded becomes the knock you offer.

You're not weak for asking. You're wise for surviving. Strength is not silence, it's connection. One human hand reaching out to another. Sometimes the bravest sound in the world is that soft knock echoing through the hallway of your pride.

Emergency Moves

If asking feels impossible, start small. These steps can quiet the noise of fear long enough to let courage through. Not knowing doesn't always mean you're lost; sometimes it means you're still, waiting for life to find its rhythm again.

- **Start close:** Ask a trusted neighbor, friend, or coworker who knows your situation. Proximity builds empathy.
- **Be clear:** State what you need: "I need food for three days," "a ride to work," or "$40 to keep the power on." Specific asks invite solutions.
- **Trade if you can:** Offer babysitting, cleaning, or cooking. Barter turns help into a partnership.
- **Protect your dignity:** Accept what lifts you, never what makes you feel small.
- **Write it down:** Track who you asked and what was offered. Gratitude builds future community.
- **Give back when ready:** A thank-you note or a shared meal repays the spirit of the knock.

PART IV

FROM BROKE TO BREATHING

This is the turning point. You're no longer counting hours until the next check, you're counting moments that feel like living again. The panic that once gripped your chest loosens, replaced by a slow, cautious calm. It's not wealth, it's breath. This part isn't about comfort; it's about remembering that control, dignity, and peace were never lost, only buried beneath fear. Now you begin uncovering them, one deliberate choice at a time.

When the storm quiets, the silence feels strange. You keep waiting for another call, another notice, another blow, but sometimes, nothing happens. And that's the miracle. You've paid what you could, talked through what you couldn't, and learned the difference between crisis and inconvenience. Breathing space returns like light through blinds: thin at first, then steady. You're not "fixed," but you're free enough to think again.

Freedom, at this stage, looks like small wins: the first time you fill your fridge without panic. The first night you sleep without checking for overdraft alerts. In the first month, you pay bills early rather than late. These aren't luxuries, they're quiet revolutions. They prove that progress doesn't always shout. Sometimes it whispers, *You made it through.*

Now comes the rebuild, but not the kind sold in seminars. It's slower. Wiser. More human. You've learned that money is motion, not meaning. That dignity comes before dollars, patience before profit. "Enough" is a moving target, and peace lives in the pause between survival and striving.

Part IV isn't about fixing the past. It's about shaping what comes next: saving, forgiving, resting. Each is progress. You're not racing anymore. You're pacing. You're learning that breathing is its own form of success.

No one warns you about what comes after the crisis, how strange it feels to live without danger. The quiet can feel empty at first. But that emptiness is the space, the margin you fought for where life begins again.

You start noticing what money can't measure: sunlight on the kitchen table, the taste of coffee without worry, the sound of laughter returning hesitant, then real. These details don't erase what happened; they prove you've reentered life. You rebuild not because the world changed, but because you did.

Maybe you still owe. Perhaps you still stretch. But you no longer mistake the bill for your worth. The same mind that once scrambled for survival now plans for possibility. You write goals in margins instead of debts. You talk about next year instead of just next week. Being broke was never only financial; it was a spiritual constriction. Breathing again means reclaiming space to imagine.

In this new light, you become a different kind of rich: rich in clarity, self-respect, and the patience hardship forged. You don't romanticize struggle, but you recognize its gifts: discernment, empathy, endurance. You can hear desperation in another's voice and know what to say to help them hold on. That's wealth, too.

The rebuild isn't a finish line; it's a rhythm. You'll still tighten, still stretch, still worry sometimes. But fear no longer decides who you are. You do. And that quiet authority, the one you earned in darkness, will carry you farther than any paycheck ever could.

You didn't just survive the fall; you learned how to rise without forgetting what the ground felt like. Every hard choice, every empty night, every dollar stretched taught you to listen to your own strength. This is what recovery looks like when it's real, not loud, not perfect, but alive. Take a breath. You've earned it. The same resilience that brought you here will build whatever comes next.

CHAPTER 17

THE FIRST BUFFER — BUILDING YOUR $500 LIFELINE

When you don't know what to do next, start by building a margin, a space between panic and planning. That's where choices begin to breathe again.

Five hundred dollars. It doesn't sound like freedom, but it is. It's the difference between panic and breathing, between watching the gas gauge in fear and knowing you can still get to work tomorrow. For millions, $500 is the thin wall between stability and collapse. Once that wall is built, you start to rest. It's not wealth, it's oxygen.

You've already learned to stretch meals, juggle bills, and outthink scarcity. Now comes the step that turns reaction into readiness. The first buffer isn't about becoming rich; it's about not breaking. It's the moment you decide that emergencies no longer get the final word.

Why the First $500 Matters

That first small cushion is your proof that control can return. Five hundred dollars may not change your world, but it changes your posture inside it. It gives you time to breathe before choosing, time to solve rather than scramble. Every dollar saved is a little silence where panic used to live.

Angela began with twelve crumpled dollars from the bottom of her purse. She hid them under the sink, promising not to touch them unless the lights were about to go out. The following week, she added eight from skipped snacks, then two from helping an elderly neighbor clean her porch. By the end of the month, she had thirty-seven dollars. When the gas bill arrived, she didn't cry; she planned. For the first time in years, she met a crisis with calm.

That calm changed her rhythm. She named the jar *Peace Money* and taught her children to drop coins in whenever they could. The jar was small, chipped at the rim, but heavy with purpose. "It's for the days that scare us," she said. Each deposit felt like pulling a brick out of fear and placing it in safety.

Start Smaller Than You Think

Most people never start because they think saving means hundreds of dollars. It doesn't. Start with what's within reach. Skip one habit that doesn't feed or protect you: a snack, a ride, a small subscription. Walk when you can. Cook double and freeze the leftovers. Each skipped cost becomes a coin of control. Some weeks it's two dollars. Some, none. But each act tells your future self: *I'm still steering.*

If your income is unpredictable, try the "one-in-ten" rule: every tenth dollar belongs to the buffer. Ten percent sounds like a mountain until you see it one coin at a time. Over months, the trickle becomes a tide.

The beauty of starting small is that it builds confidence. You stop feeling helpless and start noticing progress, even in pennies. You begin to celebrate invisible wins: the times you wanted to spend but didn't, the moments you chose future peace over present comfort. That mindset, not the jar, is what changes everything.

Separate and Protect

Keep your buffer where temptation can't reach it, a jar, envelope, prepaid card, or digital wallet with a password you never memorize. The separation is the shield. Money mingled with grocery cash and rent evaporates. Money marked *do not touch* grows roots.

Two small examples prove the point. One single dad kept his envelope taped behind a photo of his kids; it reminded him why he couldn't spend it. Another woman opened a digital wallet titled *Not Today, Fear.* Naming it turned saving into resistance.

If someone in your circle is struggling too, invite them to start beside you. Accountability turns isolation into routine. Check in weekly: *"How's your jar?"* A quiet partnership keeps you honest. And when one of you dips into the fund, the other reminds, *"That's what it's there for. Just rebuild right after."*

Turning Small Wins into Peace

When the jar hits fifty dollars, celebrate quietly. When it reaches one hundred, hide it better. At five hundred, pause. Feel the difference in your shoulders. A flat tire no longer feels like a collapse; it's just a delay. That's the sound of stability: soft, steady, earned.

You don't need a miracle. You need a margin. That first buffer *is* your margin, proof that survival can evolve into strategy. It's the first real breath after months of holding your chest tight. Later, you'll look back and realize the hardest part wasn't saving it, but believing that *small could be enough.* But it is. Every coin and crumpled bill whispers the same truth: *you have the power to create calm inside chaos.*

Emergency Moves: Build Your $500 Lifeline

Here's how to start building that first financial buffer, your lifeline right now:

- **Name your goal:** Label it *"$500 Lifeline."* "Names give direction and meaning.
- **Separate it:** Keep it far from spending money. Out of sight, out of reach.
- **Start small:** Even one dollar counts. Repetition beats amount.
- **Use the one-in-ten rule:** Save one out of every ten dollars you earn.
- **Sell with purpose:** Turn clutter into cushion, not just cash.
- **Guard the fund:** Use it only for real emergencies: rent, heat, food, transport.
- **Refill fast:** Whenever you dip into it, rebuild right away. The lifeline must stay ready.
- **Track growth:** Write down your total each month. Seeing progress builds discipline.

CHAPTER 18

SMALL SPARKS — TURNING GIG CASH INTO STABILITY

Once you've built a small buffer, the question becomes: how do you keep it alive? For many, regular income alone isn't enough to grow savings quickly. That's where small sparks matter, those little moments when effort unexpectedly earns a bit more. It might not feel like much, but those sparks are how you move from barely surviving to quietly building stability. They remind you that forward motion is still possible, even when progress seems invisible.

Sometimes you circle back not because you failed, but because the uncertainty is teaching you what certainty really feels like.

Why Small Sparks Matter

The gig life is rarely comfortable. It's uncertain, irregular, and often unpredictable. Yet within that uneven rhythm lies the power to regain control. You might walk dogs, sell baked goods, clean cars, repair phones, teach a skill online, or run errands for neighbors. The work itself matters less than what it represents: your ability to generate income without waiting for permission. Each side job is a quiet act of defiance, proof that you can still create options when systems ignore you. Over time, those scattered earnings add up to something bigger than money: self-trust.

Start with What You Know

One woman began cleaning two apartments a month with her niece. At first, it felt like survival disguised as work, but by the fifth month, her weekends had purpose again. The cash helped, but what mattered more was the movement. She no longer ended the week defeated. Word spread, and soon she had five clients, each one earned through kindness and consistency. "I used to feel replaceable," she said. "Now I feel needed." That was her first real raise, disguised as dusting.

Grow from What You Have

Another neighbor started selling banana bread at the weekend market. In the first week, she earned $20; in the second, $40. By the third month, her small kitchen had become a quiet workshop of hope. She didn't call it a business; she called it breathing. "I can't fix everything," she said, "but I can bake something." Her rhythm kept food on the table and fear out of her chest. Each loaf reminded her that stability could rise from her own hands.

Protect the Flow

Each side's effort brings freedom, but that freedom fades without structure. When gig money arrives, give it direction before it disappears: half goes to needs, 30% to your $500 lifeline, and 20% toward growth supplies, repairs, or tools that make the next job easier. That small discipline turns hustle into stability. Keep gig cash separate from regular spending. Use a jar, envelope, or prepaid card. Seeing your work become a visible stream of income builds pride and persistence. Over time, this habit rewires how you see money not as something slipping away, but as something that can finally follow your lead.

Turn Lessons into Leverage

Every gig teaches something if you listen closely. Some drain you; others build you. The key is reflection. Write down what worked, what didn't, and how each made you feel. Which efforts brought peace instead of pressure? Which ones could grow into something steadier? Patterns reveal sustainability. Awareness becomes your compass, transforming survival into a system. And when you share what you've learned, offering advice to a friend or posting tips online, you turn experience into currency. Teaching what helped you once becomes another spark.

From Motion to Momentum

She now calls her weekend earnings "quiet money." It doesn't shout, but it saves. It bridges the space between stress and stability. And when that gap begins to close, something shifts, and you stop bracing for disaster. Stability doesn't begin with abundance; it begins with motion. Protect that motion fiercely. The more you honor the work that steadies you, the faster those sparks turn into fire. And when they do, you'll recognize the feeling, the same calm you felt when your jar hit $500, the sound of your life finding its rhythm again.

You've already done the impossible: survived what once felt unlivable. Now comes the part no one teaches: remembering your power. You've shown that stability isn't handed out. It's built, day by day, with tired hands and relentless hope.

This is where consistency quietly replaces crisis, not with noise or applause, but with rhythm, routine, and the steady proof that you can hold what you've built.

The next chapter doesn't belong to survival. It belongs to you.

CHAPTER 19

WHEN REST BECOMES WORK — FIGHTING BURNOUT WHILE YOU BUILD BACK

Momentum feels like strength until it starts costing more than it gives. After weeks of hustling, saving, and rebuilding, fatigue shows up dressed as discipline. You wake up tired, push through the ache, and call it commitment. But exhaustion isn't a badge of honor; it's a warning light on the dashboard. Rest isn't surrender. It's a strategy. Without it, the foundation you're rebuilding won't hold, no matter how determined you are to keep moving.

The Lie of Endless Grind

Burnout hides behind pride. It tells you to push through, grind harder, and never slow down. It whispers that stopping means failure, that rest is a luxury you can't afford. The lie spreads easily because it appears convincing. But exhaustion doesn't build it; it blurs. A tired mind overreacts, overspends, and overlooks what's obvious. You can't spot opportunity when your body is begging for a pause. The grind doesn't make you disciplined; recovery does. A healthy rhythm sharpens your focus and restores direction. Burnout turns effort into noise.

The Wake-Up Call

A single mother working night shifts learned this the hard way. She'd come home just as her kids were waking up, forcing a smile through the fog of sleeplessness. One morning, she fainted at the stove, her body made the decision her pride refused to. The hospital stay that followed became her first real rest in years. When she returned home, she drew hard lines: no double shifts, no calls on Sundays, and bedtime before midnight, no matter what. Her income dipped at first, but her life began to stabilize. "I thought I'd lose everything if I slowed down," she said. "But slowing down is what saved me." Her story spread through her workplace. Soon, schedules shifted. Her pause permitted others to breathe.

The Body Keeps the Receipts

A warehouse worker in his fifties said it best: "You can't outwork your body. It keeps the receipts." For years, he clocked twelve-hour shifts, proud he never missed a day. Then his hands began to tremble, and he couldn't hold a wrench. Forced to take a week off, he slept ten hours a night for six straight days. That rest didn't make him weak; it made him capable again. The body doesn't punish; it remembers. Every skipped meal, sleepless night, and ignored ache becomes a debt eventually paid in recovery. Now, he takes lunch outside under the same tree every day. "It's only twenty minutes," he said, "but it resets everything." That ritual became his repair.

When Identity Starts to Fade

Burnout isn't just exhaustion; it's an erosion of identity. You stop laughing. You stop trusting your limits. Even joy feels heavy. A teacher once said, "I didn't stop caring because I stopped loving my work. I stopped caring because I couldn't feel anything anymore." That's the quiet collapse exhaustion causes; it steals your ability to connect. When your body and mind are drained, even victories feel hollow. The fix isn't guilt; it's rhythm. Rest must be part of the rebuilding process, not a reward for finishing it. Learn to recognize the early signs: irritability, confusion, persistent worry. These aren't flaws, they're messages. Listen before they turn into alarms.

Boundaries as Survival

Schedule stillness the same way you schedule shifts, and protect it as fiercely as you protect your paycheck. Even thirty minutes of quiet, carved out in chaos, can reset an entire week. Don't call it a break. Call it a boundary. Boundaries don't limit you; they preserve you.

A retired mechanic once said, "If you don't rest by choice, you'll rest by force." His force came after a heart attack. He rebuilt differently: less overtime, more walking, no apologies for saying no. "Now I treat sleep like a side gig that pays in years," he said.

That mindset isn't indulgence. It's insurance. Recovery isn't an interruption to progress; it's the fuel that makes progress possible.

Paying the Health Debt

Your body is a ledger. Every act of forced endurance is a withdrawal, and at some point, the account runs dry. You can't build anything lasting while borrowing from your health. Pay the debt back: hour by hour, meal by meal, boundary by boundary.

Recovery isn't idleness. It's a strategy. A quiet hour. A slow meal. Music that steadies your breath. A walk without headphones. These aren't escapes, they're maintenance. They return you to the pace that built you in the first place.

Five minutes of stillness can restore what five hours of panic can't. You didn't come this far to stay exhausted. You came to reclaim peace. Rest doesn't pull you off the path; it keeps your feet steady on it.

Emergency Moves

- Treat rest as currency. Budget it like money.
- Schedule recovery. Write it down. Protect it like rent.
- Watch your signals: Dread, irritability, forgetfulness = past due.
- Use micro-rests. Five minutes of silence can reset your system.
- Nourish, don't numb. Sleep, stretch, hydrate. Substances delay the crash.
- Guard your boundaries. "No" is a safety tool, not an attitude.
- Replace guilt with discipline. Recovery is a skill, not a weakness.
- Create a ritual. End each week with one act that restores: reflection, gratitude, or stillness.

CHAPTER 20

THE SLOW RISE — BUILDING A LIFE THAT DOESN'T BREAK AGAIN

The morning is quiet, no sirens, no alarms.

Healing isn't a comeback; it's construction. It unfolds one steady layer at a time, long after the noise of collapse has faded. The slow rise begins when you stop measuring progress by speed and start measuring it by stability. You learn that consistency outlasts adrenaline.

When you don't know how fast to move, slow down, give wisdom a chance to catch up. Confusion isn't weakness; it's a speed limit designed to protect you.

After a crisis, the urge is to rebuild quickly, to return to what feels familiar. But quick fixes break down just as fast. The better path is quieter: plan, test, reinforce, rest. A roof built overnight won't survive the next storm. A life rebuilt slowly will. Speed makes headlines; steadiness builds homes.

Proof One: Rhythm - Showing Up for Yourself

The first sign of recovery is rhythm. You begin showing up for yourself the way you once showed up for everyone else. You pay bills on time. You cook instead of skipping meals. You clean the sink before bed, not for perfection, but because you promised yourself order.

The slow rise is built on small, repeated victories that no one claps for but you.

A former EMT once said, "After years of emergencies, the hardest thing was learning not to live like one." He began walking instead of running, eating instead of gulping, and listening instead of reacting. The shift was simple, yet profound: he stopped chasing peace and started designing it.

Rhythm builds reliability. Once the noise quiets, movement returns in measured beats, allowing for enough sleep, responding to messages slowly, and learning to trust silence again.

Proof Two: Boundaries - Guarding What You've Rebuilt

Once rhythm returns, the next lesson is protection. Rebuilt lives need gates that open and close with intention. You decide who has access to your time, your energy, and your quiet. You learn to separate urgency from importance and realize that most of what shouts is neither. When someone says, "It'll only take a minute," you remember that every minute is an investment.

A young baker recovering from debt discovered the real lesson wasn't how to make more money, it was how to spend less energy on the wrong things. "Now I bake fewer cakes, but they're better. I deliver less, but I sleep." Her business grew because she stopped over-serving everyone who asked.

Boundaries aren't walls; they're gates. They protect what peace has built.

Proof Three: Patience - Letting Growth Catch Up

Growth that lasts moves slowly enough for your character to keep up. Quick gains collapse because they don't give your habits time to mature. You can't rush wisdom, balance, or peace. The slow rise protects you from the high cost of fast success.

Patience is a quiet kind of strength. It doesn't show off; it holds steady until you're ready to receive more.

An older carpenter who rebuilt his shop after a fire said, "It took two years to get back to where I was, but this time I understand every nail." That's what patience teaches: mastery through repetition, confidence through waiting.

A hurried life may look productive, but it's fragile. The steady climb lasts because every step knows where it's going.

Proof Four: Gratitude - Turning Survival into Story

The fourth proof is gratitude, not the performative kind, but the grounded kind that keeps you tethered when life begins to speed up again. Gratitude for breath, a roof, work, a friend, a chance. It doesn't erase pain; it gives it proportion. Gratitude turns survival into a story, transforming what once hurt into what now holds you steady.

A bus driver rebuilding after bankruptcy said, "I don't need to win anymore; I just need to keep." That's wisdom earned through struggle, the understanding that sustainability is the new ambition. Gratitude steadies what hustle once shook. It reminds you that enough can finally be enough.

The slow rise isn't glamorous, but it's sacred work. It's how strength becomes gentleness and ambition becomes endurance. You don't bounce back, you build forward. And this time, the foundation remembers everything that nearly broke you.

When the world rushes, resist. When your mind demands more, breathe slower. There's no finish line for peace, only practice.

You used to run from silence; now it's where you rest. Exhaustion once proved effort; now peace proves progress. You no longer chase belonging; you build it, brick by steady brick. To rise slowly is to rebuild wisely.

Emergency Moves

- **Start small** – Repair one habit at a time; permanence beats momentum.
- **Protect rhythm** – Keep sleep, meals, and movement consistent.
- **Audit commitments** – If it drains more than it gives, release it.
- **Reinforce wins** – Track progress weekly; repetition builds strength.
- **Practice stillness** – Schedule it before stress schedules itself.
- **Value patience** – Speed ruins what peace repairs.
- **Revisit purpose** – Ask often: *Does this align with the life I'm building?*
- **End the week with reflection** – What stayed steady? What needs adjusting?

Recovery isn't the end. It's the beginning of the rebuild.

CHAPTER 21

THE LIVING LEDGER — KEEPING WHAT YOU'VE REBUILT FROM BREAKING AGAIN

Even when you don't know what comes next, awareness is still a form of action. The pause before the next move isn't a delay; it's part of the rebuild.

Peace once proved progress, but now it asks for presence. The air is still, but your body remembers the weight it once carried. Every rebuilt life holds a silent ledger not of debts and dollars, but of lessons and limits. The balance shifts daily: energy in, energy out; peace gained, peace lost. Those who stay standing learn to read that ledger before it's overdrawn.

The hardest part of recovery isn't rising, it's staying risen. You can rebuild strength, habits, and hope, but maintenance asks a deeper question: Can you protect what you've earned without letting fear take the lead?

Stability isn't a finish line. It's a practice that keeps breathing.

Discipline One: Awareness - Reading Your Energy Ledger

Track what costs you most, not in money, but in attention. The hours given to arguments, the minutes lost to scrolling through noise, the evenings consumed by worry, it all goes somewhere. Every choice either feeds your stability or drains it. Awareness is the first form of wealth.

A grocery clerk recovering from burnout shared her rule: "If it costs me my peace, it's too expensive." She began counting rest as income and stress as loss. Her budget changed, and so did her life. Peace became her currency.

Another man kept a small notebook labeled *Energy Spends*. Each night, he tracked where his attention went. "Argued = minus 10 points. Walked outside = plus 15." It sounded simple, but within a month, he noticed patterns and stopped giving his calm to people who didn't reciprocate.

The ledger wasn't about perfection; it was proof that balance becomes visible once you decide to measure it.

Discipline Two: Prevention - Guarding Before It Breaks

The second discipline is prevention. Problems caught early don't become collapses. It's not paranoia, it's stewardship. Check your energy the way you'd check your bank account. Low balance? Deposit quietly. Overspending? Withdraw from chaos. The same calm that protected your $500 buffer now protects your boundaries.

A young father rebuilding after a divorce learned this the hard way. "I used to measure love by sacrifice," he said. "Now I measure it by sustainability." He stopped overpromising what his peace couldn't afford. His relationships didn't shrink; they deepened. Boundaries didn't push people away; they taught them how to stay.

Prevention is humility in action. It admits you're not unbreakable and checks the warning lights before smoke appears. Fatigue isn't a flaw; it's a signal. The wise treat it like an early bill: the sooner you pay attention, the less interest it costs you.

Discipline Three: Renewal - Scheduling Peace Like Maintenance

The third discipline is renewal. Everything from work to purpose, faith, and even joy requires periodic maintenance. Renewal isn't starting over; it's updating what still matters. The strongest people aren't those who never fall apart; they're the ones who schedule restoration before the breaking point returns.

A hospital janitor with forty years of service put it best: "You don't clean the floor because it's dirty. You clean it because it's used." Life is the same. Maintenance isn't punishment, it's respect for what you've built. What you maintain externally, in your work and rest, must reflect the story you tell yourself internally.

Protecting your rebuild also means guarding your narrative. The story you tell yourself becomes the blueprint you live by. Stop saying *I'm still recovering.* Start saying *I'm maintaining.* Language isn't decoration, it's architecture. Words either hold walls up or let them fall.

Even peace needs tending, like a garden that survives only when watered with awareness. You'll feel guilt for saying no, discomfort when slowing down, and temptation to prove you're still productive. That's when it's time to check your ledger again. Ask: *Am I living from balance or depletion?* If depletion wins, stop. You've already lived that chapter, don't repeat it out of habit.

The living ledger isn't about perfection; it's about attention. You'll overspend on some days. You'll forget to rest. You'll fall behind on peace payments. The difference now is that you'll notice sooner and recover faster. That's progress that sticks.

A retired bus driver once said, "I thought survival was strength. Turns out balance is." That sentence is the summation of the ledger. The math is simple: protect what you've paid for.

Maintenance doesn't mean stillness; it means steady motion, aligned with purpose. The life you've rebuilt won't protect itself. You protect it by choosing presence over panic, rhythm over rush.

And when the world begins to pull again, when exhaustion whispers like an old friend, open the ledger. Look at the entries. Remember how long it took to climb out. Then close it, take a breath, and maintain your balance.

To maintain is to honor the rebuild to prove that peace can last. Peace doesn't disappear when life gets noisy; it simply waits for you to notice it again.

Emergency Moves

- **Audit energy daily** – Ask: What did this cost me? What did it give back?
- **Guard peace like property** – Not everyone earns access.
- **Check for early cracks** – Fatigue, resentment, and dread are warnings, not flaws.
- **Schedule renewal** – Maintenance prevents collapse.
- **Watch your words** – Speak in terms of stability, not survival.
- **Protect rhythm** – Keep your foundational routines sacred.
- **Balance emotional books** – Don't invest in what doesn't return care.
- **Revisit your why** – Stability stays strong when tied to purpose.

CHAPTER 22

THE QUIET PROOF — WHEN YOU NO LONGER HAVE TO EXPLAIN SURVIVAL

One morning, you'll wake up and realize you didn't start the day in fear. No account check. No mental math. No apology to yourself for not being further along. You'll sit for a moment, and the quiet will feel strange because it's safe.

That's when you'll know you've crossed into something real.
Not wealth. Not escape.
But peace that doesn't ask for proof.

No one around you will notice the shift. You'll still buy groceries, pay bills, and check the weather. But somewhere between those small tasks, you'll feel the weight of survival turn into steadiness. You'll breathe, and it won't feel like work.

You'll stop rehearsing your explanations: why you struggled, why you failed, why you stayed. You'll understand that survival doesn't need an audience. It's not performance. It's proof.

Proof that you endured what most people can't imagine and came out not rich, but real.

Poverty taught you things comfort never could: how to stretch a day, how to listen to your body, how to keep moving even when you had no map. That wisdom doesn't fade; it just stops running the show.

The people who never saw your fight will see your calm. They'll think it came easily. You'll smile, knowing they'll never understand how many quiet miracles it took to reach ordinary.

And that's okay. You're not here to retell pain. You're here to live what came after it.

You've learned that life doesn't need to be loud to be full. That survival isn't shame, it's skill. And that the things that almost broke you gave you the patience to live more slowly, more deeply, and more truly.

You are not behind. You are not broken. You are not waiting for the world to understand.

You've built something no one can repossess, peace that lives inside you.

That's the quiet proof. The kind that needs no headline, no validation, no applause.

The kind that whispers, *I made it, and I'm still here.*

You don't owe anyone your story. You've already lived it.

And now, finally, you can rest in what you've built, a life that doesn't shake when the wind blows.

When Survival Turns to Strength

You've done what most never have to do: rebuild yourself amid collapse. You've faced days that don't make headlines, the ones where you had to pretend everything was fine when it wasn't. You stood in silence that could've swallowed you, yet you found a way to speak anyway.

That's not luck. That's a strength.

Strength isn't what lifts cars or carries mountains. It's what lifts you out of bed when everything inside says, *Stay down.*
It's counting coins when your pride says *Don't.*
It's answering the phone you fear, making the call you dread, opening the envelope you've avoided for weeks.
It's surviving when the world forgets to notice.

The truth is, no one teaches us how to keep going when everything falls apart. But you've learned it here.

You've discovered that survival isn't just about reacting, it's about creating. Every act of endurance was a step toward building something greater: self-trust, self-worth, and self-definition.

The world told you money measures value. You've shown that resilience does.

Now, as you stand at the edge of what's next, remember.
You don't owe anyone proof of how hard it was.
The fight itself was proof enough.

What you owe yourself now is peace, not permission, the kind that grows quietly when you stop apologizing for existing.

You started this book searching for something to cling to when everything fell apart.

What you found wasn't a map, it was a mirror.

The person who made it here proves you were never truly lost.

You're allowed to rest. You're allowed to laugh again. You're allowed to build slowly, gently, on your own terms.

The pressure that once defined you can no longer hold you back. You've stretched beyond it. You've turned struggle into skill, and pain into pattern recognition. You now know how to survive anything, and that knowledge is freedom.

So breathe. The work isn't to start over; it's to move forward.

What you've carried has already shaped you into someone unbreakable. You are proof that even in ruin, something beautiful continues to grow.

You are evidence that endurance becomes strength, and when strength softens, it becomes peace.

You made it through the part where everything broke.
Now comes the part where you live.

NOTES & SOURCES

This book was written from lived experience, field research, and verified community and nonprofit data. All examples, case studies, and composite stories are drawn from real survival experiences and adapted to protect privacy while preserving truth.

Statistical & Program References

U.S. Bureau of Labor Statistics (BLS) – *Consumer Expenditure Survey* and *Household Income Data*, 2023–2024.

Federal Reserve Board – *Economic Well-Being of U.S. Households* Annual Reports.

Pew Research Center – Financial Security and Inflation Impact Studies.

U.S. Department of Housing and Urban Development (HUD) – *Emergency Rental Assistance Program* Data.

U.S. Department of Energy – *Low-Income Home Energy Assistance Program (LIHEAP).*

National & Community Resources

211.org – Nationwide hotline for food, shelter, utility, and crisis support.

Feeding America – National network of food banks and community pantries.

National Low Income Housing Coalition – Rent assistance and housing rights.

Consumer Financial Protection Bureau (CFPB) – Tools to avoid payday loans and debt traps.

The Salvation Army & Catholic Charities USA – Emergency relief and utility aid.

National Suicide Prevention Lifeline – Dial 988 for 24/7 confidential support.

Inspirational & Educational Influences

Barbara Ehrenreich – *Nickel and Dimed: On (Not) Getting By in America* (Metropolitan Books).

Matthew Desmond – *Evicted: Poverty and Profit in the American City* (Broadway Books).

Tressie McMillan Cottom – *Thick: And Other Essays* (The New Press).

Bell Hooks – *All About Love* (HarperCollins).

Mariame Kaba – *We Do This 'Til We Free Us* (Haymarket Books).

Acknowledgment of Composite Examples

Characters such as Angela, Malik, Rosa, and Tasha represent composite experiences gathered from interviews, public forums, and confidential correspondence. Their stories reflect patterns shared by thousands navigating financial precarity, each altered slightly to protect identity and integrity.

Citation Note

All cited data and program descriptions are drawn from public or government sources listed above. Readers seeking current eligibility criteria or funding updates should refer to the official websites or regional offices of the relevant organizations, as policies may be subject to change.

RECOMMENDED READING AND FINANCIAL AID RESOURCES

This list extends the conversation beyond these pages. Each title and resource below offers a way to deepen understanding, rebuild stability, or connect to help that lasts longer than a crisis.

Recommended Reading – Understanding Money, Work, and Survival
Barbara Ehrenreich – *Nickel and Dimed: On (Not) Getting By in America*
Matthew Desmond – *Evicted: Poverty and Profit in the American City*
Tressie McMillan Cottom – *Thick: And Other Essays*
bell hooks – *All About Love*
Sonya Renee Taylor – *The Body Is Not an Apology: The Power of Radical Self-Love*
Vicki Robin – *Your Money or Your Life*
Michelle Singletary – *The 21-Day Financial Fast: Your Path to Financial Peace and Freedom*
Tanya Van Court – *Goalsetter Guide to Generational Wealth*
Tressie McMillan Cottom & Roxane Gay (eds.) – *The 1619 Project: Essays on Power, Labor, and Equity*

Financial Aid and Assistance Programs

211.org – Nationwide hotline for food, shelter, and utility help.
Feeding America – Find food banks and community pantries by ZIP code.
Modest Needs Foundation – Small emergency grants for workers living

paycheck to paycheck.

Operation HOPE – Free financial coaching and credit counseling.

National Foundation for Credit Counseling – Certified nonprofit debt-management support.

LIHEAP (Low-Income Home Energy Assistance Program) – Utility-bill assistance and weatherization programs.

HUD (U.S. Department of Housing and Urban Development) – Emergency rental and housing resources.

The Salvation Army & Catholic Charities USA – Local emergency financial assistance.

Black and Brown Economic Alliance – Entrepreneurship, housing, and financial literacy initiatives.

Single Stop – One-stop access to government benefits, tax credits, and college aid.

Workforce, Income, and Stability Resources

CareerOneStop.org – Federal job and retraining portal.

Goodwill Career Centers – Free resume, job search, and certification programs.

UpTogether – Peer-based community grants for families building financial resilience.

Fiverr Learn & Coursera – Free and low-cost online skill certifications to build a flexible income.

National Urban League – Employment, housing, and community support initiatives.

AFTERWORD / AUTHOR'S NOTE

I didn't write this book to sound wise.
I wrote it because I've been broke enough to know that advice doesn't feed you, and theory doesn't keep the lights on.

This book was born out of panic nights when the balance in my account felt like a ticking clock. I remember the dull ache of pretending everything was fine, staying calm while the world quietly unraveled around me. I remember the silence after the last dollar left, when even breathing felt expensive.

I wrote this for that person, the one holding it all together with tape, hope, and muscle memory. The one who doesn't need a lecture, just a light.

If this book has done what it was meant to, you already know this: you were never the problem. Poverty might shrink your options, but it doesn't shrink your worth. Struggle may have bent you, but it also trained you. It gave you precision, empathy, resourcefulness, and patience lessons no comfort could teach.

You've learned how to stretch time, how to find kindness in small places, how to create something from almost nothing. That's not a weakness. That's mastery.

I still have days when fear knocks. It hasn't vanished, it's just lost its authority. But each time I breathe through it, I remember: survival gave me something wealth never could, a truth that doesn't flinch.

So if you're reading this with a tight chest and a future that feels small, hear me now: you're already doing the hardest part. You're still showing up, still trying, and still choosing not to quit.

You don't owe the world an explanation for your struggle, your pace, or your healing. All you owe yourself is the chance to keep going slower, steadier, smarter this time.

And one day, not far from now, you'll look around and realize something simple but profound:

You built a life that doesn't break when the money runs out.
That's what I call wealth.

ACKNOWLEDGMENTS

To the person holding this book, thank you for making it to the end. You could've turned away. You could've said, "Not today." But you didn't. You stayed with it, and with yourself. That means more than I can say.

Every word in these pages came from a place I once stood: unsure, tired, and still trying. If even one sentence reached you when you needed it, then it did what it was meant to do.

To the people who remind me what real strength looks like, my family, you are the quiet rhythm behind every line.

And to the one voice that never stopped pushing me toward honesty: James Baldwin. His words taught me that truth doesn't have to shout to be revolutionary. I tried to carry that kind of honesty here.

Finally, to anyone still in the middle of the storm, this book isn't a promise that life gets easy. It's a reminder that *you* do.

Thank you for reading, for enduring, and for proving that survival, when held with grace, becomes a form of art.

Will

ABOUT THE AUTHOR

Carl Williams is a veteran and educator who began writing three years ago to help people find steadiness when life breaks without warning. His work centers on rebuilding with honesty, dignity, and the quiet strength of small, steady acts.

He is the founder of *Inkylines & Words*, a Black-owned independent bookstore and creative press that publishes stories of resilience, belonging, and the power of starting again.

Carl lives in Japan with his wife and two sons, continuing to write for those learning to stand, breathe, and rebuild one day at a time.

You can discover more of his work at:

https://payhip.com/inkylinesandwords

An Inkylines & Words LLC Publication
Yokohama, Japan | Honolulu, Hawaii
https://inkylinesandwords

www.ingramcontent.com/pod-product-compliance
Lightning Source LLC
LaVergne TN
LVHW100327210926
848480LV00003B/1284